DIET TRICKS

HEAVYWEIGHT WAYS TO USE YOUR BRAIN AND BEHAVIOUR
TO LOSE WEIGHT … AND KEEP IT LOST!
(AND TO ACHIEVE LOTS OF OTHER THINGS TOO!)

PART 1: BITE-SIZED
WEIGHT-LOSS TIPS

MARK BIDDISS
"DR MARK": COGNITIVE-BEHAVIOURAL
COACH AND MENTOR
(AND SUCCESSFUL WEIGHT-LOSER)

A COGNITIVE-BEHAVIOURAL APPROACH TO CONTROLLING
YOUR WEIGHT

DR MARK MEDIA

First published in Great Britain in 2020
by
DR MARK MEDIA

A CIP catalogue record for this book is available from the British Library.

Cover illustration: Antonina Tsyganko/Shutterstock.com

ISBN 978-1-905441-44-0

www.DietTricks.com

A Dedication

I think for me to personally dedicate such a book as this to a particular person will be received by them in much the same spirit as would be received from me a can of antiperspirant deodorant, fresh-breath spray or anti-stinking feet powder. It could be interpreted that I think they need it. So rather than risk hurting the feelings of any given individual, I will instead dedicate this book and the associated website to all those people I care about who are unhappy with their enlarged body-shape, and who have failed in the past to successfully lose the weight they'd really like to lose and keep it lost. You know who you are; this book is for you. Please read it. Enjoy.

Contents – *The Menu*

(*W*) – means applicable to weight-loss ONLY

Bite Size Weight-Loss Tips

1. **You Need to Recognise Why You Got Fat**
   Diets Fail Most People
   Obstacles and Barriers
   Use Your Mind to Overcome Obstacles
2. **Don't Put it Off**
3. **Aim for Enjoyable Lifestyle Changes**
4. **Don't Deprive Yourself**
5. **Start Off Gently**
6. **Record Everything About Your Eating and Exercise for One Month Before Dieting**
7. **To Start Off, Don't Change What You Eat Too Much – Just Reduce the Amount**
8. **Counting Calories Can Constrict You** (*W*)
9. **Learn How to Cook Simple Meals for Yourself** (*W*)
10. **Don't Eat Too Much Highly Processed Food** (*W*)
11. **Snack Between Meals if You Feel the Need** (*W*)

A Polite Disclaimer

The cognitive and behavioural tools in this guide can be extremely effective and powerful in helping you with practically any sort of behavioural change. This is especially true if you use several tools at the same time. For this reason you must be very careful in how you use and apply them. I take no responsibility whatsoever if you use any of the tools in unhealthy or inappropriate ways beyond the scope of my instructions or guidance.

A Very Serious Health Warning!

STOP Right Now if You Think You Might Have an Underlying Health Condition

DO NOT use any of the cognitive or behavioural tools in this guide if you have – or even *think* you *might* have – an eating disorder of some kind. If so, you need professional help beyond the scope of this weight-loss guide. So please seek medical advice first.

You probably have such an eating disorder if any of the following statements describes you:

- You have a just about continuous obsession with food, dieting, your weight, or appearance, often to the exclusion or detriment of other important aspects of your life.
- You think you look fat when everyone you ask says you look thin.
- You already weigh much less than what is thought to be healthy for your body-type and height.
- You have a history of severe under-eating.
- You overdo exercise with the main aim of keeping your weight down.
- You often binge-eat, make yourself vomit after eating, or use laxatives inappropriately.

If even just one of the above statements describes you, please consult your doctor or a mental-health professional for help if you haven't already. Please DO NOT use any of the tools in this guide unless a medical professional who totally understands your condition says it's okay to do so.

Also, please DO NOT use any of the tools in this guide to lose weight if you have a dietary or health condition that could be affected if you restrict your diet, such as if you are a pregnant woman or someone suffering from a blood-sugar or blood-fat disorder. The same goes if you suffer from *any* underlying chronic health condition or if you are taking medication which influences your metabolism. If you have any doubts whatsoever, please seek medical advice first.

YOU HAVE BEEN WARNED!

Preface

This is not the sort of diet book you are usually served. I won't be telling you to drop a certain food group or only eat on days with the letter "e" in them, or anything like that. I won't be giving you recipes or suggesting specific exercises.

Instead, I will reveal all the things I learned about and found useful in helping me to overcome the various obstacles and barriers to successfully losing weight and keeping it lost. This book will give you scientifically sound tips and techniques that will help you stick to whatever diet or weight loss regime you are following. As you probably know, most dieters give up their diet, or if they do lose the weight they want, they put it back on quite quickly. But the tools that helped me involve simple changes in behaviour, thinking and reasoning that everyone can do, and, if carried out properly, they can help you be one of the few people who succeed in losing weight for good. Many of the tools literally trick you into thinking and behaving in more useful ways, helping you to overcome patterns of thinking and behaving which have stopped you from successfully losing weight until now.

And, as the book's subtitle implies, many of these tools can be used in other areas of life as well.

I'm Not a Medical Doctor

I want to make it totally clear right here and now that I am not a medical doctor or a medically-trained psychiatrist, and have absolutely no pretentions or claims to such status.

As you will discover in the introduction to this book, my credentials for writing it are based partly on my own personal experiences of successfully losing weight, and partly on my deep, personal interest and research into the practical applications of the cognitive and behavioural sciences to everyday living.

I do have formal training and qualifications in Cognitive-Behavioural Coaching and Mentoring (and Neuro-Linguistic Programming) and, as a result of this, I am registered as a Member of the Institute of Counselling, based in the UK, as a practising Cognitive-Behavioural Coach and Mentor.

And, I am a doctor in the academic sense, having a PhD in Physical Science. I have been known professionally by the name "Dr Mark" since the late 1990s, in my education consultancy work, in my science and maths books, CDs and DVDs for teachers, and on my "Dr Mark" website: www.Dr-Mark.co.uk.

Perhaps most significantly here, since 1996 I have spent much of my academic career teaching people about the scientific process, how we use it and what we can learn from it.

All of this helped me on my own weight-loss journey and has given me the background to offer the weight-loss tools in this guide to you, too.

So get started and prepare to enjoy a meal of easy-to-swallow ideas that will help you lose the weight you want.

Scientific References

All of my weight-loss tools and tips are evidence-based, founded on scientific research and theories, and are consistent with the ideas behind the cognitive and behavioural sciences generally. So throughout this whole guide you'll hear me use expressions such as "studies show " or "the evidence suggests that" when I'm about to tell you about a useful tool.

But you will soon notice that I have included very few references to any specific scientific research. The main reason I didn't bother to include references is because practically nobody ever bothers to follow them up. I'd guess that less than one percent of general readers bother at all; probably as little as one in every several thousand readers, if that. Rightly or wrongly, in wisdom or folly, nearly all general readers are more than happy enough to trust the written word of the writer. It's usually only the seriously geeky, anorak researchers like me who bother to follow up references in books, and then only the odd one here and there rather than every single one. And the main reason I do this is to get more details about the particular bit of research quoted, sometimes to see if I agree with the conclusions of the researchers and the writer, rather than to see if the writer is telling fibs by making it up.

So, for the benefit of people like me, I plan to gradually put on my website (http://www.DietTricks.com) the various scientific references to the weight-loss tools and tips. If you should come across a particular weight-loss idea in my guide for which you'd like to see the formal scientific support, and can't find it on my website, then please do feel free to email me for it. I will, of course, do my very best to oblige.

What's in the Guide

(Do not skip this bit: it's important – and it may save you from a lot of reading!)

Why Is this Called Diet Tricks?
You Might Not Even Need to Read More Than *The Menu*
How Is this Book Laid Out?
The Full Weight-loss Guide
So What Exactly Is on the Diet Tricks Website?
Ways to Use the Guide
Dr Mark's Top Ten Tips
You Can Use the Tools in this Guide to Achieve Other Things

Losing weight, and keeping it lost, is really hard for the vast majority of people. But you probably knew that already. As likely as not, you found out for yourself. It's probably why you're looking at this guide now.

Diets don't work. At least that's what many people think. Although it's not strictly true that diets don't work, we do need to be honest with ourselves here: losing large amounts of fat by following a diet is really difficult for the *vast majority of people*. And assuming they succeed, keeping the fat off in the long-term is practically impossible for all but a tiny few. In other words, for all sorts of reasons, almost everybody fails to lose weight and keep it off in the long-term, regardless of whatever old or newfangled diet they follow. Worse still, the chances are that both you and me come under the category of "the vast majority of people".

There's loads of scientific evidence and survey results to back this up, so there's no denying it. The fact is, if you go on the sort of diet that almost everyone opts for, the chances are you're highly likely to fail, and you're quite likely to end up even fatter still. As I say, those are the facts.

But don't despair; have hope, even. Because the main reason that the vast majority of people fail to lose fat and keep it off on the long-term is that they simply don't do things properly; more often than not following very poor advice, or a lack of good advice. In other words, it's not so much that the diets themselves fail, but more because people fail to stick with the diet for various reasons, usually because they haven't been taught properly how to.

There's no doubt that slimming down requires a degree – often a really good degree, it's true – of persistence, determination, courage and willpower or self-control. But such things are not always in good supply when we most need them, especially good old willpower or self-control. In fact, relying on willpower alone is simply not enough for most dieters, as is evident from the failure rate.

Regarding willpower, we have two obvious options here:

1. Increase the strength of our willpower, which is do-able, as I'll show you;
2. Do things in such a clever and devious way that we don't need to rely so much on willpower in the first place, if at all.

For instance, if you find that doing something is enjoyable, or if you can learn to enjoy it, then you don't need to use willpower to do it. Similarly, if you can make a desired healthy behaviour into an automatic *habit* – like the habitual routine of brushing your teeth – then you won't need to rely very much, if at all, on willpower. In other words, we can use our brain and behaviours to help us reduce the amount of willpower or self-control we need to eat less, and maybe to exercise more, too. For example, we can learn how to motivate ourselves more and form healthy new lifestyle habits. These are just some of the really useful and practical things you will learn about in my guide.

But this guide is not just about strengthening or bypassing your willpower, or motivation, or making and breaking habits, though we will look at all these. In fact, this is probably unlike any other diet book you've ever read before, assuming you've ready any, that is. I know a lot of writers have said this about their work, but you'll soon see why I've said it.

It is first and foremost a book full of scientifically-sound, evidence-based, effective cognitive and behavioural tools and techniques that will help you reach your goal-weight. But to give credibility and "weight" to the contents, I've woven in my own personal story here and there. Where it's relevant, I'll tell you about how I battled and tackled being overweight – or just plain fat – why I wanted to lose the fat, how I finally got motivated to lose it, the many things I tried to help me to lose it – including what worked well and what didn't – and how I eventually got healthily slimmer at long last. In other words, this is at least partly an autobiographical account about my own sometimes tortuous journey from being too fat to getting slimmer. But my main reason for telling you about me is to give you examples of how to use and apply many of the cognitive and behavioural tools. I do promise though not to bore you to death with my story, at least I'll try not to. I will keep it brief and relevant, and mostly on the Diet Tricks website, anyway.

In reading this guide, my hope is that you will learn many ways of thinking, feeling and behaving which have been proven in studies to be effective for many, many people in helping them to lose weight, including me. In a way, this is a guide that describes and evaluates lots of these tools and techniques from my own point of view, but shows how they might be effective for you too. So that's why I will tell you what I tried, how scientists think it works, how effective it is supposed to be, and often I'll tell you how well, or not, it actually worked for me. I will also be taking a little bash at any techniques that I think are not much good and why. At the very least, I will offer you cautionary advice or maybe another point of view on how they might not work for you, or how you might change them to make them work better.

Why "Diet Tricks"?

That's a good question, as it might sound as if it's got something to do with the sort of tricks you see in stage magic. And, to some extent, that's not far from the truth. Most stage magic tricks work using sleight-of-hand, props or some other way of misdirecting you or deceiving you to make you perceive (that is, think, feel, experience) or even behave in a certain way. Well, most of the diet tricks in this guide can be thought of as working in a similar way on your mind. What I'm referring to as "tricks" here are effective, novel and sometimes even a bit strange ways of *deliberately* and *purposefully* thinking, feeling and behaving which you can use to help change things in your life. And just like stage magic tricks, many of the clever cognitive and behavioural tricks I'll tell you about almost certainly work at least in part by slipping under the filtering radar of your conscious mind to more strongly act upon your unconscious mind. And it is your unconscious mind which influences and drives so many of your thoughts, feelings and behaviours in your everyday life, usually unbeknownst to you.

Initially I was mostly interested in tricks to change the way you think, feel and behave around eating (and exercise) to help you lose weight. So that's how this book of "diet tricks" evolved. In fact, I've included twelve cognitive (thinking) and behavioural tricks from my very first research in the final chapter of this book, as you'll see. And there are lots more in the more detailed information in Part 2 of my Diet Tricks guide, accessible on the associated website (www. DietTricks.com).

You Might Not Even Need to Read More Than *The Menu*

You'll be pleased to know that you don't even have to use all of this book to help you lose weight, especially if you'd really rather not. In fact, you can get a lot of really useful tools and tips to use immediately *just* by reading carefully through *The Menu* (the Contents Page) alone, without the need to read any further; honestly.

To make my point I insist that right now, this very second, you flick back a few pages and read right the way through all the *numbered* titles in *The Menu*. Go on – the whole lot will probably take you no more than about two or three minutes; then come back here when you've read through it.

Done it? See what I mean? Hopefully, I've just proven to you that you even now know a lot of great tools to try out – *just* by reading through those titles, and probably without the need to read any more about a given tool if you understand what to do. For instance, Remind Yourself Daily Precisely Why You Want to Lose Weight (tool 19) and Eat Slowly and Mindfully (tool 64) are quite clear instructions as they stand, I'd say, and you may already know pretty well what to do to apply them yourself without needing any further explanation or advice from me, or certainly no more than the Bite-Size Tip explanation I provide for each in this book. Fair enough if so.

On the other hand, the Bite-Size Tips are just that – bite-size instructions for easy digestion. Each of these short tips usually only gives you just the bare bones of what you need to do – enough information to use it effectively, but little or no explanation about why or how the tip works. But that may well prove more than enough for you to work with, of course, and it's also why I only included the bite-size tips in this volume.

You probably noticed that there is a handful of tips in *The Menu* which don't make much sense as they're written there, perhaps that even sound a bit cryptic to you – such as Use Back From the Future Thinking (tool 47) and Think "Doublethink" (tool 49). So these few do require you to at least read the relevant Bite-Size Tip in this book if you want to know what to do.

It's also true that a few of *The Menu* items tell you *what* to do, but it may not be clear *how* to do it – such as Get More Motivated (tool 52) or Learn to Tolerate Hunger, Desire and Craving (tool 59). Again, you'll need to read at least the relevant Bite-Size Tip if you want to know how to do these things.

Mainly, *The Menu* is just that, a list of offerings, not a full meal itself. For some people, even the Bite-Size Tips in this book won't make a three-course dinner that will fill them up with cognitive and behavioural techniques for keeping weight off. To get to the meat of the matter such individuals will need to consume more from the associated website.

How is this Book Laid Out?

You'll see from *The Menu* pages that there are 78 numbered entries. These are the 78 weight-loss tools, techniques or tips I want to give you that tell you how to use your brain and behaviour to help you lose weight, and keep it lost. Just as promised in the subtitle of this book. Actually, there's a lot more than 78 tips buried within this guide, dozens more, in fact, especially if you use the associated website, but I've chosen to go with 78 headings, or main tips.

You'll also see that I've divided these 78 main tips into five sections:

Starter Tit-Bits (tips numbered 1 to 20)
Topic 1: Losing Weight Has to Matter a Lot to You Personally
    (tips 21 to 30)
Topic 2: What is Your Weight-Loss Goal? (tips 31 to 44)
Topic 3: Navigable Obstacles and Barriers to Losing Weight
    (tips 45 to 66)
Twelve More Tricks of Thinking and Behaving That Can Help
    You Lose Weight (tips 67 to 78)

A Note on Order

As you read through this guide, you might think that some of the tips are more important than others and should have been listed earlier in the book. The important thing for me was to put the four main sections in the right order: Starter Tit-Bits, Topic 1, Topic 2 and Topic 3. These do follow a natural order. Beyond that, most of the tips themselves are not meant to be in any particular order of priority. The main reason for this is that what may be an important and useful tip for one person may prove to be less so for another. I have certainly found this from my own experience and from people I have spoken with about it. In any case, the tips and tools mostly appear in the order in which I wrote them.

The Full Weight-Loss Guide

In the end, I divided the full, big fat weight-loss guide into three parts.

This book is *Part 1 – Bite-Size Tips*. This book contains all the information you need on the Starter Tit-Bits (tips 1 to 20), followed by brief descriptions of the rest of the tools (tips 21 to 78). These tips may be short but they still give you useful information. I say "Bite-Size" Tips but, to be fair, some are pretty big "bites", which you might need to chew a bit before "swallowing". That said, most are no more than a page or two in length – many much shorter – and shouldn't take you any more than two or three minutes to read.

Now, it is quite possible that you might want more detailed guidance than what is in this book, including even more tools and more explanation from me, based on both my own personal experience and on scientific research. In this case, you'll find much more information in *Part 2 – Bigger Portions to Help You Even More* and *Part 3 – Why You Eat the Way You Do* on the associated website: www.DietTricks.com.

So What Exactly is on the Diet Tricks Website?

First of all, you'll find all the information in this book also on the website, in both text and audio-podcast formats.

I'm a massive fan of audiobooks and podcasts myself, having listened to hundreds of each over the years. And I know I'm not alone, which is why I wanted to include them in this guide. Audiobooks and podcasts are great for learning, and, as well as being enjoyed while sitting comfortably in a chair, they can be listened to when travelling, cooking, gardening and exercising, to name just a few other options. The plan is to provide you with audio versions of everything written on the website, plus loads more over time. I may also be making some videos, which will be available to be viewed online, so keep an eye out for them, too.

But what about Parts 2 and 3 of the Guide? Well, Part 2 consists of bigger portions, containing much more detailed information about tools 21 to 68 that are summarised in this Part 1 book. Just as in this book, you'll see one "chapter" for each tool on the website. I'll tell you right now that some of those individual chapters on the website run to the equivalent of only a page or two of text, but some go to many pages, such as those about willpower and habits.

The longer chapters almost always contain a lot more tools and tips for you to try out as well, so you may find it worthwhile reading through them carefully, especially if you don't feel that you've been satiated enough by the bite-size tips in this book.

Part 3 is *Why You Eat the Way You Do.* This section of the guide is over and above the basic weight-loss tips. It's more of a background to the whole food and eating issue as it applies to you individually. Self-knowledge is important in all aspects of our lives, especially in helping us to achieve things. In the process of writing this book, it occurred to me that it was really important – and potentially useful – to understand what makes us eat the way we do, from both a physiological point of view as well as a psychological one. For instance, I wanted to look at what sort of eater I was: one who responds mostly to my body's metabolic needs, or more to my emotional needs? I was also interested in precisely why I get hungry in the first place: what are the biological and psychological mechanisms which make me feel the sensation "hunger"? And I wanted to know why I found it particularly challenging to resist eating too much sugary and fatty food. I would argue that knowing something about all these things as they apply to you can help with your weight-loss journey. In turn, this understanding of yourself can help you prepare for and overcome some of the inevitable obstacles and barriers you will face.

For your interest, I've included in the back of this book a more detailed chapter breakdown of what you can expect to find on the website for Part 2 and Part 3.

And, as I said in the Preface, the website is the place to look if you want to follow up any of my references to the scientific studies that form the basis of my tips and tools.

More "Fat but Fit?" Information on the Web

I wanted to see if I really could be "fat but fit", as the saying goes, just in case I failed to lose the weight I needed. That said, I was actually pretty confident that I could lose the fat I wanted to lose, especially as I learned and started to apply more and more of the tools I tell you about in this guide. But the "fat but fit?" question is still really important, especially for those overweight people who are simply unable to shift their excess fat, for whatever reason. They need to know the health implications, and what they can do to minimize the potential risks to their health regardless of their weight.

I had originally planned to include all my findings about this thorny question in this Part 1, but because I didn't want this book to get any bigger, I decided to include just a brief summary of the "fat and fit?" question, and then put the full details on my website, instead. You can read the summary of: Can You Be Fat and Fit? appended to Bite-Size Tip 22: You Need to Really Want to Lose Weight Badly Enough in this book.

Subscribe to the Website for Further Updates

My plan is to add extra material to the website from time to time – especially new, research-based cognitive and behavioural tricks which you might find useful. I'm also looking at a range of products and services that I may offer to help people achieve their desired weight-loss more easily.

So to keep updated about such things, as well as to access the FREE material on the website, please subscribe. It's totally FREE, and rest assured that I most definitely WON'T bombard you with newsletters and marketing emails, I won't share your personal information with anyone at all, and you can unsubscribe at any time. But I WILL send you the odd email – no more than one or two each month – always with some useful and totally FREE resource of some sort as well as any news; I promise! And, if I do decide to change anything about the way I send my emails, you'll still be able to opt-out easily. I promise that too.

The website address can be found on other pages of the book, but just so you can have it again, you can subscribe at http://www.DietTricks.com.

Ways to Use the Guide

You could, of course, start out by reading and committing to use all 78 of the Bite-Size Tips in this book. Depending on how fast you read, this will probably take you about two or three hours. This alone will give you a great box of tools to help you use your brain and behaviour to lose weight. Interestingly, the editor of this book told me that just working through the text seems to have had the effect of influencing her to get more serious about her own eating, drinking and exercise habits. She's stopped putting things off and now has a definite action plan to eat and drink less, and exercise more. So it can work!

But, if you are keen to learn more, you could then read or listen through all the detailed chapters in Part 2 and Part 3 of the guide on the website. That would take you a lot more time, of course, but you would without a doubt have a formidable armoury of tools to use to help you lose weight and keep it lost.

On the other hand, another good approach could be to read all the Bite-Size Tips in this book, and, if you want more instructions and tools for a particular weight-loss tool, then read or listen to the associated chapter in Part 2 on the website. I still recommend going through much of Part 3 as well at some point, if nothing else just to get a better understanding of why you eat the way you do.

Perhaps the quickest thing you could do is make a note of all the tools you read in *The Menu* which strike a chord with you, and that you think you'd definitely be willing to try. Then read the Bite-Size Tip for each one in this book and see if you have enough information to get on with. If not, read the bigger chapter in Part 2 on the website to get as much information as you can about it. And as I said a moment ago, parts of Part 3 will be worth a read too, when you get a spare few minutes.

Dr Mark's Top Ten Tips?

Actually, this is a really, really hard one for me, because I reckon all the tips in this guide are Top Tips. But if you really threaten me with something unspeakable, force me down on my knees, and compel me to give you *only* my Top Ten Tips which have been proven to pretty much help *anyone* lose weight, regardless of things like age, gender, what sort of eater they are, or the sort of weight-loss programme they choose, then here they are, in the same order as they appear in the guide:

- Tip 3: Aim for Enjoyable Lifestyle Changes

- Tip 4: Don't Deprive Yourself
- Tip 19: Remind Yourself Daily Precisely *Why* You Want to Lose Weight
- Tip 21: Keep an Accurate Record of Everything
- Tip 25: List All the Consequences of Losing Weight and Being Slim (especially to you personally)
- Tip 27: Expect to Make Long-Term Lifestyle Changes
- Tip 44: Your Weight-Loss Goal Statement Should Stimulate Multi-Sensory Thinking and Emotions
- Tip 45: Identify the *Navigable* Obstacles and Barriers
- Tip 48: Plan in Advance to Replace an Unhelpful Triggered Behaviour With a Helpful One
- Tip 66: Ask For Help if You Need It

And remember please: I only listed the above 10 tips because you forced me to by threatening me with something unspeakable, on my knees, no less; *I* didn't want to do it. I actually think you should go through everything in this guide to see what works best for you personally, even if you only read through all of the Bite-Size Tips in this book. I think you should only limit yourself to the above list if you really don't have the time or energy to go through the rest. That's my advice, anyway. Take it or leave it.

Repetition and Contradiction

As you read through the various tips, you will occasionally notice what, at first sight at least, appears to be repetition in the text and even apparent contradictions between certain weight-loss tips. Please don't fret about this.

Apart from errors on my part, the repetitions are usually deliberately intended to reinforce something I'm telling you, aid your understanding, aid your memory or to remind you of something relevant I told you elsewhere. I accept that you personally may find such repetition unnecessary and maybe even a bit irritating now and again. I apologies to you personally in advance if so, but, based on my years' of experience as an educator to people of all ages, I felt that some people would benefit from such repetition, if not you. So please bear with me.

As for the apparent or even seemingly blatant contradictions you may spot here and there, I merely report to you what the cognitive and behavioural scientists found out in their weight-loss studies and experiments. Moreover, the fact is, we strange humans sometimes do indeed think, feel and behave in seemingly contradictory ways; I know I do. Likewise, many of us have apparently contradictory aspects to our personalities; again, I know I do. But my use of the words "seemingly" and "apparent" is important here, because a weight-loss tip may "seemingly" or "apparently" contradict another, but it probably does so only in certain specific circumstances or situations, and thus may not contradict in others. Furthermore, you may well discover that these "seemingly" or "apparently" contradictory weight-loss tips both work just fine for you, even when used together. My advice is to give them the benefit of the doubt and give them a try to see if they work for you.

You Can Use the Tools in this Guide to Achieve Other Things

You may remember that part of the over-long subtitle of this guide is: "… (and to achieve lots of other things too)". That's because this book is all about how to achieve change in your life, and how to achieve it using your brain and behaviours; hence the first part of the subtitle. In case you haven't noticed, the focus of this guide is on weight-loss, and so I wrote all of the tools from that point of view.

You might also have noticed a capital "W" written in brackets after twenty-nine of the numbered tools in *The Menu*, such as after Counting Calories Can Constrict You (tool 8), and Consider Weighing Yourself Daily (tool 33). This means that particular tool is only really relevant for helping you to lose Weight, and is not much use for anything else in your life. But that means the remaining tools – without the "W" – can be used to help you achieve other things in your life as well, as long as you can work out for yourself how to apply them, which shouldn't be too difficult at all in most cases. You just need to be a bit creative with your thinking on how to use a given tool for whatever else it is you want to achieve.

Introduction

Who is this Guide For?

Well, let me start by telling you who this book is not for.

First and foremost, it's not for you if you are looking for some easy, quick-fix diet instructions and guidance; such things simply don't exist, so good luck with that one.

Nor is it really meant for people who have one of the rare cognitive or physical conditions that for genetic, mental or physical reasons cause them to store too much fat. That's not to say that such individuals will not find the tools and techniques I describe useful and effective for them; they may well do. However, as far as I know, my tips have only really been tried and tested properly on people with more "standard" bodies and metabolisms, for want of a better term. So such people who *don't* have so-called "normal" bodies and metabolisms, and who do have one of these rare conditions I allude to, should seek medical advice before embarking on any weight-loss approach, be it mine or anyone else's.

Nor is my book meant for people who believe in ideas such as the "Law of Attraction", which claims that you "attract" fat merely by your very thoughts! If that's what you believe, my guide is not for you.

No, my book is for you if you are overweight or obese, and accept that – aside from genetic influences (blame your parents) – eating too much food really did cause you to put on weight, assuming that you have a pretty standard body and metabolism. In other words, you accept that you are overweight because you put too much food and drink down your gullet, and probably don't exercise enough. Moreover, it may well be the case that, like me, you've tried losing weight before with no long-lasting effect, and would like to learn some new ways that might help you to get it right this time around; all that yo-yoing is exhausting.

Of course, you may be one of those rare overweight people who are genuinely happy with your enlarged body shape, or simply couldn't care less either way. Good for you if so; there really is no reason whatsoever why you should not be happy with how you look, whatever your shape – I would strongly argue that it's the person inside that matters, anyway. And I really do mean that; I'm not into "body shaming" in any way.

However, even if you really are happy with the way your body looks or couldn't care less, I would draw your attention to the well-known potentially negative health implications and the serious risks of carrying more than your fair share of body fat, especially around your belly. That said, I suppose it is possible that you are already fully aware of this and are simply not bothered about it either. Fair enough if so. Mind you, I suppose if all this applies to you it's extremely unlikely that you'd be reading this weight-loss guide in the first place.

So this guide is for people who are currently overweight (a.k.a. fat) and would like to learn some new and effective tools and techniques to help them lose the fat, and who believe that it is possible for them to do so, because it is. This guide will also be useful if you're already on a weight-loss diet or programme, and are perhaps not finding it as easy to stick to as you would like. This guide is also for you if you've already lost the weight you want, but would like to learn some ways that will help you stay slim, which is one of the toughest things to do for many people.

Of course, you might not want to control your eating and exercise habits to help manage your weight; instead you might want some ideas to help you manage your intake of certain foods or drinks for other health reasons, such as coping with diabetes or high cholesterol.

I suppose it is worth mentioning that this book might also be useful for you if you are trying to increase your weight. My thinking here is that you might simply try doing the opposite of what many of the various tools and techniques suggest, or use them to increase your fat reserves rather than decrease them. It would be worth a try, though I won't be concerning myself with that personally.

What I'll be Telling You, and What I Won't Be Telling You

As I said right at the beginning, in this guide I will *not* be telling you what you should weigh or should not weigh, what to eat or what not to eat, or what fat-shedding exercise programmes you should or should not do. Those are covered in thousands of dieting and exercise books, and on zillions of websites.

No: my idea was to write an account of the scientifically-proven tools and techniques I found to be effective, or not so effective, in helping me stick to my own personal eating and exercise choices, and how they might f help you stick to yours.

I will also aim to clear up some of the myths of dieting as I go along, and offer my perspective on some of the common questions people want answers to, such as: How often should I weigh myself? How much weight should I aim to lose each week? Do I need to both eat less *and* exercise regularly if I want to lose weight? Can I rely on exercise alone to lose weight?

I won't go as far as saying that I offer you some sort of "weight-loss system", although my guide could easily enough be used as that, and as such would almost certainly prove effective overall. Moreover, it has to be said that you may not find a particular tool or technique noticeably effective or even appealing to you personally, or, perhaps it only works in a very small way. That said, you may discover just one single tool or technique that proves particularly powerful for you, and thus makes all the difference to your slimming success, and so you may choose not to even bother with any others. Stranger things have happened.

No Detailed Food Advice Here

As I've said, apart from obvious advice about not eating too much sugary, fatty, and pre-processed foods, I won't be giving you any detailed advice about what you should or shouldn't eat. That's not what this book is about, and, as you will discover, I personally don't recommend calorie- or unit-based diets anyway; just good, healthy eating generally, with lots of variety. There's literally thousands of diet books and websites out there which will give detailed advice about what foods to eat and what not to eat, if you want such advice. Nor am I qualified to do so anyway, not being a trained nutritional therapist – I have enough on my plate as it is, thanks very much. Again, there are well-qualified people out there, and you may benefit from seeking the advice of one once you've decided how you want to go forward, and if you think you could use personalised advice about what you should or shouldn't eat.

In any case, most people have at least some idea about the sorts of and amounts of foods which can easily make them get fat, which is why I confine myself to just saying watch out for the fatty and sugary foods you eat, and keep processed foods such as ready meals and reconstituted meat products to a minimum. But eating too much of almost any food can make you fat, however healthy the food itself is. In fact, I know of some fat people who eat perfectly healthy food, but they're fat because they simply eat too much of it.

That's why I confine myself to just offering cognitive and behavioural tools and techniques you can use to help you eat less and more healthily generally.

Guaranteed to Work?

All of the tools and techniques in my guide are based on scientific evidence, have been tested in one or more studies, and all have been found to work for many people in the studies concerned.

However, it's important for you to realise that rarely does a tool or technique work for absolutely everyone in a study. It's more accurate to say that it worked for the *majority* of people in the study, to some extent. Well-run scientific experiments on real Human Beings, in real-life situations, almost always show simply the percentage of people in the study who found the technique worked to a greater or lesser extent for them.

Moreover, a study may have been conducted only on a very specific group of people, such as from a particular age-group, weight-range, gender, ethnicity, geographic location, or socioeconomic group; factors which may possibly be relevant to the study results. And such a study group may not necessarily represent or apply to you personally.

So when I suggest you try a tool or technique, what I'm saying is that, based on the research, you are *more likely to be successful* if you use that tool, than if you do not. And because we're all a bit different one way or another, I will also suggest that you play around a bit to see what works best for you. In other words, a tool may not work for you, even though it has worked for most other people who've tried it. It's just the nature of being the unique creature that you are. And that's one reason why I've put in many different tools and techniques for you to try: hopefully you *will* find at least some of them useful and effective for you in losing weight.

What I'm offering you is a wide and varied range of cognitive and behavioural ideas which, individually, can each contribute at the very least a small benefit to you, but together, using as many as possible together as I suggest, will, because of the cumulative effect, almost certainly make you far, far, far more likely to be successful in your slimming endeavours, if not quite guaranteed. That promise I will make.

Why Should You Listen to Me?

Good question. Well, the most obvious answer is that I was quite fat for a very long time – borderline obese at one stage, apparently. I not only had to struggle to lose weight from time to time, but I also found it really hard to maintain that weight loss; a classic yo-yo dieter, no less. Even then, I never managed to get down to a really good healthy weight. So, unlike some writers of weight-loss books – who shall remain nameless – and as you will learn about me in these pages, I really do know the emotional pain and anguish of being fat, and how hard it is to lose weight and keep it off.

For instance, I know what it's like to give in to the urge to binge eat; I know what it's like to go to a restaurant with friends with the intention of having just a healthy main course, only to give in and have a starter, a dessert and maybe a not so healthy main course either; I know what it's like to scoff more when I feel bored or a bit down emotionally, as well as when I've just received a bit of great news; I've lost count of the number of times when I've given in to the wish to take one too many biscuits from the pack and then, thinking that since I've now already gone over my limit anyway, think "what the hell" and just polish off the whole pack. The same goes for the ice cream tub. And the cheese tray. And the box of chocolates. And worst of all in all this, I know how emotionally crap I feel afterwards for giving in. In other words, I've been there, done that and worn the X-Large t-shirt. But here's the good news: I did succeed in slimming down in the end using a range of brain- and behaviour-based tools and techniques that I want to tell you about in this guide.

And that is not all you need to know about me if you want to have faith in what I am going to tell you. As I said in the Preface, I am actually a trained scientist, with a First Class Honours Degree and PhD, both obtained, I am proud to tell you, from University College London, UK – without doubt the finest university in the whole multiverse (though you might accuse me of being a tad biased here). As for my day job, as well as being an independent science and maths education consultant, presenter, trainer and author (see www.Dr-Mark.co.uk if you are interested), I'm also trained in Cognitive-Behavioural Coaching and Mentoring and even in Neuro-Linguistic Programming (NLP), which does have one or two useful tools and techniques for cognitive and behavioural change. I've also written *An Introduction to Coaching and Mentoring for Teachers* course guide, which you can find in several schools, along with my other "Dr Mark" science and maths books for teachers, which have nothing to do with this weight-loss guide.

As a dyed-in-the-wool, healthy-minded, agnostic sceptic, since 2005 I've had a particular keen interest in learning and researching evidence-based tools and techniques – consistent with the cognitive and behavioural sciences – that can help me and you work out and achieve what we really want in life. To that end, as well as trying to keep my finger on the pulse of latest research and developments, I have built up my own reference library of well over one thousand books, scientific journals and audio-visual lecture programmes, and will continue to add to it. I've even read and listened to some of it as well. So I like to think that I am quite well qualified to write this guide, whatever way you look at it.

My Fat Story: About Me and My Fatness

If you're not really that interested in my story – which is reasonable enough, I suppose – I suggest you skip this section. That said, you might well find some of my experiences apply to you too, and so you might benefit from hearing my story.

Still here?

Well, I think I should make it clear that apart from a very short period in the late 1980s when I was about three stone overweight, I've never otherwise been significantly or clinically obese as such, though not that far off. In other words, I was never quite so fat that when I stood on the scales they read, "Only ONE person at a time, please!", or "Sorry, I do not weigh elephants" (though I do think that I almost heard the scales scream out in pain once). Nor did I have more rolls than a pastry truck.

The problem for me has rather been the case of being more or less overweight, i.e. fat, since my late twenties, which was back in the late 1980s. In fact, it was back then, as implied a moment ago, that I reached my maximum weigh-in at three stone heavier than I really should have healthily been, which was technically obese, I believe. So, yes, I have been obese, albeit a long time ago.

Since then it has been the usual sorry tale of yo-yo dieting and wildly fluctuating weight. For most of the time up until just a little before the writing of this guide, I've weighed in at between one-and-a-half and two stone overweight. Or put another way, putting my weight into the Body Mass Index (BMI) formula, I was just too short for my own good. One effect of this was in the shower: at my fattest, although it was not true that my belly was so big that my feet didn't get wet, it was true that I had trouble seeing either my feet (or my genitals) without leaning forward or struggling to suck my immense gut in; and that really is true. Furthermore, my oldest sister once mentioned that the men in the Biddiss family were prone to what she called the "Biddiss Bulge"; I am sure if I had let her she would have stroked or patted my rounded Buddha belly fondly like it was a sleeping cat on my lap.

What Made Me Finally Take Action to Lose Weight?

An obvious question that might come to your mind about me is: why did it take so long for me to finally get around to losing my excess body-lard and keep it lost? Good question. I think the honest answer must be that my fatness didn't seem to be *too* excessive to me somehow, and so simply didn't bother me enough. Nor did it bother my wife, for that matter. I'm fortunate, I think, to have a five-foot-ten-inch, fairly muscular and broad-shouldered body-frame, which makes it quite easy to camouflage much of my excess fat, especially when wearing certain types of clothing, and even more so in the colder seasons when I'm well wrapped up. Moreover, I was fit enough – and not too fat – to do all the physical things I enjoyed doing, such as walking in the mountains near where I live.

As an aside, I think I inherited my body frame from my dad, who, it has to be said, resembled a short, stocky, five-foot-nothing ginger dwarf with freckles, blue eyes and a large, glowing red nose, that looked like a nose-shaped strawberry squashed on to the front of his face where his nose should have been; I forgot to mention that I seem to have inherited his large, strawberry-like nose, too.

But coming back to me, it was the cumulative effect of a number of things that made me finally tackle losing the lard properly and keeping it lost: a combination of negative emotions, the need for recreational fitness and the need to not die from poor health. I'll go into all this later on.

What About My Use of that Offensive Adjective "Fat"?

By the way, you might have noticed that when talking about *my* weight and body shape I used that potentially rather offensive adjective "fat". Well, if such a word offends you then I will warn you that when I am talking about myself throughout this book I will often be using other potentially offensive "weighty" words. So you'd better brace yourself to get used to it. I am talking about *me*, after all, and a bit of tongue-in-cheek, light-hearted deprecation is no offence to me, at least.

You see, I am the sort of chap who calls a spade a spade – even if it is a shovel – and so I believe in good, old-fashioned, plain speaking. However, when I'm talking about you and other people, I will usually be much more polite and use gentle expressions such as "overweight", which is perhaps more politically correct. But the problem I have with the adjective "overweight" – often preceded as it is in polite conversation by the cringe-worthy words "a little ..." – is that when talking and thinking about me at least, "a little overweight" is just, well, too polite, too gentle and too non-confrontational for me. The adjective "overweight" – when compared to "fat" – does not help me to motivate myself enough to take any positive actions to shed my excess blubber.

It's worth pointing out too, by the way, that I'm using the word "fat" quite accurately here, since it is your fat that makes you fat, even if I am using it mostly as an adjective. To be perfectly honest with you, the adjective "fat" doesn't sound particularly polite to me either; I even wince a little when someone describes another person as being fat. But, as I said, I have noticed that when I think of myself as "fat" rather than just "overweight", I feel more motivated (ashamed? depressed?) and more inclined to do something about it.

Put it another way: which of these comments sounds more polite, sensitive, delicate or nice: "You look a little overweight" or "You look fat"? Chances are, if you think like me, then the latter comment makes you feel worse. And if it makes you feel worse, then it might just also have the power to motivate you more to do something about it – though I do concede that it might just as well drive you into depression, depending upon your mental health. Only you can know.

The other problem is that things change: a word that is acceptable now may not be later, and vice-versa, especially when it comes to the politically correct police. While finishing this guide, I read in the news that some groups wanted to ban using the word "fat" as an adjective to describe someone who is "overweight" because of its potentially negative emotional sting, while at the very same time other groups were reported as feeling equally strongly that we should "reclaim" and "embrace" the word in a positive new way, to rid it of its potentially negative emotional sting. One international slimming club even went as far as to play down or de-emphasise the word "weight" from its name and image, thinking it better to focus on "health and wellbeing" instead. I can't keep up.

Anyway, let's get on to the meat of the guide, my tips for how you can change your brain and behaviour to help you lose weight, and keep it off.

Bite-Size Weight-Loss Tips

Starter Tit-Bits

In this first section of the Diet Tricks guide, I want to offer you an initial few "starter tit-bit" suggestions which I (and many others) have found to be really effective in themselves; some I found almost essential for long-term success in losing weight and keeping it lost.

Bite-Size Tip 1
You Need to Recognise Why You Got Fat

When I finally resolved to shift my excess body lard and was pondering how I might go about it, a rather obvious question floated into my head: how did I get fat in the first place? Looking at this question is probably the best place to start a weight-loss journey.

The first clear and unsurprising answer was that I must have been eating *too much*, for *too long*. Too much, that is, for what my body needed to keep itself ticking over nicely on a day-to-day basis. Moreover, I suspected that I probably hadn't been exercising enough either. Put in simpler words, I reasoned that how much I weighed must depend on how much I ate and how much I exercised, and how much energy my body burned. That being so, I then reasoned that all I needed to do to lose the lard was eat "more healthily" – i.e. eat less fatty and sugary nosh – and, if I could, exercise a bit more to crank up my metabolism and burn more energy, and so, too, to tone up my muscles to look nice and firm as part of the bargain. Right? So far, so good, I thought, not least because it basically went along with the ideas and advice dished out by just about all diet systems and health gurus.

Diets Fail Most People

The only problem is, I then pondered, why is it that, as many studies have shown, even when people *do* manage to shed some weight, it is almost impossible for the vast majority of people to keep the fat off?

The fact is, well over 80 percent of people who lose weight eventually pile it all back on again sooner rather than later, and about half of them gain even more fat for good measure! In other words, they end up even fatter! It turns out that this "fat-rebound" effect is also true for people who manage to successfully shrink down to reach their target weight, and who manage to keep to that weight for several years. Just as intriguing, in my view, is that this fat-rebound effect applies even to people who join one of the well-known slimming clubs – where some of the "club leaders" I've seen on my research travels could do with losing a few extra pounds themselves – hardly a good advert for their club, is it!

If you think about it, these studies clearly suggest that, in the long term, dieting is at best a complete and utter waste of time, money and effort for most fat people. Even worse, it is as likely as not to result in fat dieters getting even fatter after all that pointless effort! Depressing or what, I thought!

Obstacles and Barriers

So all this got me thinking that despite people's best efforts, there must be major barriers or obstacles to losing weight that most fat people – including me – were just not seeing or accounting for in their weight-loss efforts. I soon came to learn that I was quite right – as I sometimes am about things – and that some things are, somewhat depressingly, a tad more complicated than I'd first thought. It turns out that for several reasons, the odds were stacked pretty heavily against me – and everyone else – losing weight and keeping it off in the long-term.

Actually, it's not very fair to say that diets themselves don't work, though there are some questionable ones, to be sure. I think it's fairer to say that most dieters just can't stick to them. Some might argue that pretty much amounts to saying that the diets don't work, though others, like me, might counter-argue that's just a neat way for some people to shift the burden of responsibility for failure away from the dieter onto the diet.

Either way, let's assume that as a general rule it's the dieters themselves who can't stick with their diet, rather than the diet itself that's at fault. That being so, then the really important question is, why? Well, it turns out that there are quite a few reasons why dieters usually fail, but, in essence, failure most often comes down to poor planning and implementation of their weight-loss efforts. And probably the biggest error in the dieters' planning is that they don't allow for all the obstacles or barriers or temptations they will almost definitely meet, and, more importantly still, they don't prepare to overcome these issues when they occur.

Use Your Mind to Overcome Obstacles

If you think about it, you only really have three obvious options when faced with any problem in your life's path:

1. *Remove* the obstacle or barrier or temptation from your path
2. Reduce the "size", or *weaken* the "strength" or effect of the problem so that it's easier for you to manage
3. *Navigate around* or otherwise avoid the problem altogether

And how to do these things is what we're going to explore deeply together in this guide.

It turned out that most of the obstacles to me losing weight were to be found in the way my *mind* worked at the time – specifically in the ways I thought, the ways I felt emotionally and the ways I behaved. As I said in the beginning, I am going to reveal to you all the tools I found useful to change the way my mind thought, and so change my behaviour, specifically my weight-loss actions.

Bite-Size Tip 2
Don't Put it Off

We all procrastinate and put off something we don't fancy doing. This goes as much for starting a weight-loss programme as for anything else. But dithering about, as if you are in two minds about something, actually sends a message to your mind that you are conflicted. Your mind can react in different ways according to the input it receives. Perhaps it will strengthen your efforts, or perhaps it will hinder them.

So you need to be careful about the way you think and feel if you chose to defer starting your weight-loss plans. You need a good, positive reason, and you don't want to send a negative message to your mind, such as that you are dreading starting your diet. If your mind gets the wrong message, it can unconsciously sabotage everything you try to do.

A common example here could be delaying a plan of healthy eating and exercise until after Christmas and New Year, or until after a holiday away, during which times you plan to indulge in the usual orgy of excess such occasions can involve. The danger here is that you might be sending a message to your brain that you won't really enjoy your diet because it's going to be ascetic and life-denying, and make you suffer generally, and so it's best to delay starting it until after you've enjoyed yourself pigging-out. In other words, you're telling yourself that you enjoy pigging-out more than being slim and healthy. You're also telling yourself that such occasions are only enjoyable if you do overindulge.

An example of this happened to someone I know very well. That person needed to lose about two stone in fatty weight. In late November they acknowledged the fact, but told me that they would postpone dieting until January, after the Christmas and New Year food-laden festivities. After all, they pointed out, what's the point of going on a diet on the run-up to Christmas and the New Year, when you're bound to put the fat back on again after all the food you've been eating and lack of exercise sitting about?

I gently pointed out that, if I were them, I'd start my healthier eating and exercise programme immediately, today or first thing tomorrow morning, because it sends the message to my brain that losing weight and getting fit and healthy really does matter to me. Such an attitude might even encourage me not to overindulge quite as much over the festive period, if nothing else because I would have already happily lost a few pounds and wouldn't want to slip back again. Moreover, even if I did indulge and put a few extra pounds of fat back on again over the festivities, at least I'd still be a few pounds lighter than I would have been if I hadn't bothered starting until later. It made good sense to me, anyway.

Evidently not to them, though. And worse still, they didn't start their diet in January after all, and it wasn't until the following August that they cracked on with it, after piling on even more fatty weight. If only they'd taken my advice …

Another example is a friend of mine who goes on diets regularly but never slims down; a classic "yo-yo" dieter. When we meet up for days out together, I can't help noticing all the sugary and fatty food he piles into his mouth. On one recent trip, he said that he was "taking a break" from his recently started diet while with me that day, and that he'd go back to his "harsh diet" tomorrow (his very words). In other words, he was telling me and, more importantly, his own mind, that he was suffering because he wasn't enjoying his healthier eating. Predictably, he failed miserably to lose the weight that he wanted.

What's interesting here is that those two people know me really well, so they knew all about my research, expertise and writing about weight-loss tools and techniques. But they nonetheless failed to take any of my advice or guidance, or even ask for it, even when they were finding it difficult to lose weight. One explanation is that they are just too stubborn to take advice from anyone. Another is that they didn't want to ask *me* for some reason or another, perhaps because they did know me so well. But yet another reason is because they simply didn't really want to lose weight *enough*. As I have argued elsewhere, *really* wanting to lose weight is a crucial component of success.

Bite-Size Tip 3
Aim for Enjoyable Lifestyle Changes

After much reflection – well, not actually *that* much, really – I came to accept that the reason I was overly lardy, and had been on and off (mostly on) for a good while, was a result of years and years of me eating too much and not doing enough exercise. In other words, I was fat because of the unhealthy lifestyle choices I had been making. So if I wanted to lose my excess fat and keep it lost long-term – settling on a healthy, maintainable weight-range for the rest of my life – then I was going to need to make a serious, lifelong commitment to changing my lifestyle. In particular, I would need to make some pretty significant changes to my eating and exercise habits. It quickly became clear, too, that to make major lifestyle changes, I needed to be emotionally ready for my weight-loss adventure. My reasoning here was that being thus ready would help with my resilience, willpower and motivation when things got tough.

Actually, "acting as if" you're ready can work well for some people, whether they feel deep-down that they really are emotionally ready or not. It's a cognitive-behavioural trick that can sort of kick-start the thinking and behaving you'll need to be successful. But such "pretending" does require a greater degree of resilience, willpower and motivation to be successful. It's probably worth a try though if you don't feel genuinely ready just yet but still want to start.

Anyway, I realised that I was much more likely to succeed if I could make the necessary lifestyle changes as enjoyable and as pleasurable as possible, so that I would still feel good in every way –emotionally, mentally and physically. I thought that if I found the changes too difficult, too disagreeable or too painful, then I'd be more likely to fail, probably sooner rather than later. So I decided I wasn't going to totally deny myself things I love to eat, like chocolate, cheese, biscuits or ice cream. And I was only going to do exercises that I enjoy, not ones I really detest.

It turns out that from what I've researched since – and have confirmed by my own personal experience and that of other dieters

I've known – a major key to successful, permanent, long-term and sustainable weight-loss is indeed to adopt similarly successful, permanent, long-term and sustainable lifestyle changes in your eating and exercise habits. But these changes have to be genuinely satisfying and enjoyable. Most importantly, if you can adopt healthier eating and exercise habits which you really do enjoy, then it's pretty obvious, to me at least, that you're going to find it much, much easier to stick with them forever, not least because you find them satisfying and pleasurable. Make sense?

Remember, the last story in the previous tip illustrates my point about striving to make your new healthier eating and exercise habits as enjoyable as possible, or, at the very least, no less enjoyable than how you eat and exercise now.

Bite-Size Tip 4
Don't Deprive Yourself

It's a fact that when people feel deprived of something that's important to them, they can end up feeling so unfulfilled and unhappy that they can no longer deny themselves the forbidden items. It's true about food, about cutting back on spending, about spending time with friends, about a sense of meaning and purpose in life, and about any other area of life. In weight-loss terms, this means that if you completely deny yourself foods you really enjoy, you will begin to feel deprived, and will then probably give in to your cravings for the forbidden food.

So I never advise people to totally cut out the things they love to eat, however fattening they may be – such as chocolate, cheese, pizza, biscuits or ice cream (some of my own favourites). If you're a chocoholic or cheeseaholic, for example, you'll most likely just end up craving them if you totally deny yourself the occasional or even frequent *moderate* indulgence.

Instead of depriving yourself completely, just cut down on them – learn to be satisfied with smaller amounts, and think of things like chocolate, biscuits and ice cream as occasional treats. In the case of exercise, I recommend experimenting with different ways of moving more energetically to get your heart and lungs working for their money. In the end you will find ways that are most agreeable to you. I love walking myself, especially strenuous brisk walking, which serves to get the old ticker and bellows pumping briskly too.

Don't exercise regularly in a way you hate, however healthy it may be. For example, I really don't enjoy jogging or swimming up and down a pool. If you hate some exercises, then, unless you can find a way of turning them into a habit, you'll need loads of willpower and motivation to keep at them, and so most likely you will fail, instead. You'll end up using every excuse under the sun why you won't go jogging or swimming today; you'll tell yourself that you'll just go tomorrow instead – and the chances are, it'll always be *tomorrow*.

And because one of my life mottoes is "Everything in moderation, including moderation", I believe in the benefits of letting your hair down from time to time – perhaps even one day each week or two. Eat just what you like, and forgo any strenuous exercise for the day. Slob out, snooze in bed all day, or just snuggle up with a good book or a good partner. Odd days here and there of such indulgence, or even excess, will not harm your long-term weight-loss, or your healthy lifestyle and wellbeing generally, and will probably actually enhance it all.

Consider applying the good-old "80:20 Rule" to your eating habits: 80 percent of the time you eat healthily and sensibly, and 20 percent of the time you eat pretty much just what you fancy. A practical way of applying this rule is across a given week, when you eat healthily and sensibly for six days, and eat what you fancy on the seventh day. Of course, if you want to stick *strictly* to this 80:20 Rule, it means eating sensibly on four days out of five, but the choice is yours.

Bite-Size Tip 5
Start Off Gently

Unless you need to lose weight as quickly as possible – perhaps for surgery, or maybe to squeeze into your wedding outfit or your holiday swimwear – I very strongly recommend starting off slowly and gently. Take your time to lose the lard and don't try to rush things. After all, chances are you've been fat for a good while now, perhaps even for years, so taking things easy for the next two, three or four weeks while you think things through and make plans won't really do any damage to your long-term weight-loss goals. In fact, I would argue that you are far more likely to succeed if you think things through carefully, learn *why* you are fat, why you eat the way you do, and find out things you can do to help you lose weight.

FAT FACT
Weight-Loss Surgery

Incidentally, having mentioned surgery, if you're thinking of having a procedure such as gastric banding or liposuction, don't think that you can avoid making major changes to some of your eating and exercise habits. Quite the opposite, in fact, especially if you expect surgery to work for you in the long-term. And if you don't believe me, ask the clinic you have in mind. They will confirm what I'm telling you right here.

In fact, the clinic will almost certainly tell you to start your healthy new lifestyle in the months leading up to your surgery, so that you have a chance to get used to new eating and exercise routines and a significantly different way of life. And as if that wasn't enough for you to deal with, they'll also tell you to try to lose five to ten percent of your body weight *before* your surgery. This is because the scientific research suggests that pre-op weight-loss will make the surgery easier and safer, and you'll likely recover more quickly and achieve more rapid post-operative weight-loss as well.

But however successful surgery is, it should only really be regarded as a temporary shortcut to long-term weight-loss, and will not, in itself, *cure* you of all your cravings to eat fatty and sugary foods to excess. For that reason alone, the clinic will also give you lots of good advice about how to adopt healthier eating and exercise habits. So the good news here is that if you are seriously considering having weight-loss surgery, what you will learn in this book – much of which even the clinic won't tell you about – will help you to make the whole process far more likely to be successful in the long term. So, take heart. As for me, I didn't need to have surgery, thankfully.

Bite-Size Tip 6

Record Everything About Your Eating and Exercise for One Month Before Dieting

When I finally did resolve to make the long-term lifestyle changes I needed in order to lose my excess fat, the very first thing I did, for about one month, was to record in the tiniest detail my eating and exercise habits as they were at the time, without trying to change them in any way. In my shiny new "Weight-loss Journal" I wrote down everything I ate and drank, when I consumed it, how I consumed it, with whom, why, and where. I recorded as best I could all the various forms of exercise and general physical movement I engaged in day-to-day. I paid close attention to the thoughts, emotions and behaviours that led me to eat and exercise – or not – in the way I did. In short, I made no conscious changes to my eating and exercise habits at all for the first month or so, but rather focused on the whys and wherefores of my eating and exercise habits, including the whats, the whens, the hows, and the with-whoms.

This proved to be a very valuable and revealing exercise, and I heartily recommend it to one and all.

And do you know what? Like many other people who do this detailed recording for a month or so I actually lost nearly two pounds of fatty weight without even trying!

Bite-Size Tip 7

To Start Off, Don't Change What You Eat – Just Reduce the Amount

When I set about making changes to my eating habits, I started off gently, making very few changes to the contents of my diet, and focusing more on just eating less. This is in contrast with just about every diet system I've come across, which all tell you to change the contents of your diet at once to a more healthily balanced menu, such as eating more fresh fruit and vegetables, and eating less fatty and sugary foods. However, as I said, for the first few weeks I started off by simply cutting back on the amount of food I was eating, especially the fatty and sugary things. Notice I said *"cut back"* just then; I didn't *cut out* any particular fat or sugar-laden food altogether, I just ate a little less of it.

And literally, within just a few days I was recording a small but measurable weight-loss. I managed to lose about four pounds in the first month, just by reducing the amount of fatty and sugary foods. It was only then that I looked at *gradually* swapping around foods and drinks in my regular diet, to have a healthier, more balanced, lower-fat and lower-sugar diet. The steps I introduced over a period of months included changes such as eating less pasta and more fresh vegetables. This gradual approach to changing my diet not only worked, but was also easy to do.

The reason I recommend this approach is because I reckon it gives you the biggest chance of success. You see, when someone goes on any reduced-calorie diet to lose weight, it is usually just too much to expect them suddenly to both eat less *and* change what they eat at the same time. This is one reason many people fail to stick to their diets for very long: it's too much all at once. So far better, I argue, to focus at first on just slightly reducing the *amount* of food you eat, without cutting anything right out of your diet, especially if you really love to eat it. Then, as soon as you get used to eating less, it's a really good idea to take a close look at your overall food-intake, and gradually change it to make it more healthy and balanced. This is where seeking dietary advice from a nutritional therapist could prove valuable; even just a single session might be worth the investment.

Coming at it from a different angle, some might argue that if you realize that you're eating an unhealthy, unbalanced diet, such as eating too much sugary, fatty and highly processed foods like "ready meals" and not enough fresh fruit and vegetables, then it might be easier to focus on making your diet more healthy and balanced, without actually eating less, at least initially. I'm sure that can work, too, and it may be worth a try if you don't fancy the idea of eating less. This also assumes, of course, that just a simple and healthy rebalancing of your diet, without actually eating less, will do the trick, which it may well do if you don't eat too much anyway. In which case we could have another diet tip here; let's call it Bite-Size Tip 7.5. But without wishing to put a damper on it, the problem is that I can think of several fat people I've known personally who did already actually eat good, healthy food, but they just ate too much of it, which is why they got fat in the first place. In their cases, all they had to do was reduce the amount of food they ate.

Bite-Size Tip 8
Counting Calories Can Constrict You

I lost all my weight *without* counting calories or food "units". Instead, as well as exercising, I just ate more healthily, cut down on sugary and fatty foods, and slightly reduced the amount of food I ate until I reached my target weight. Like me, many people have found this approach really effective. In fact, studies have shown that calorie- or unit-based diets often don't work for many people, especially in the long term.

That said, it's only fair to say that counting calories does, in fact, suit some people. Comparing the calorific value of different foods and drinks can perhaps help you to choose what changes you might like to make, especially early on in your weight-loss endeavours.

But for me personally, I find that diets based on counting calories or units are just too much hassle. They need too much measurement and monitoring, and they restrict my food choices too much.

I think the main reason I found the non-calorie-counting method successful is because I can eat absolutely anything I want on a given day, or even over a few days. This is because, even though I weighed myself daily to help keep me focused on my weight-loss endeavors, I was *primarily* focused on achieving my weight-loss *over time*, usually from one week to the next, rather than day-by-day. In other words, as long as I saw my weight slowly but consistently reducing week-by-week, I was happy, even if it did occasionally go up and down a bit day-by-day. The important thing for me was to see a downward trend over a period of a week or more. So, if I did overindulge on a given day, as long as I didn't keep overindulging on too many following days, this didn't make any difference to my weight-loss progress in the long run.

The same goes for my weight maintenance now. I've learned to eat more or less the right amount of food to keep my weight steady *over time* regardless of precisely what I eat. If I eat a bit too much on the odd day here and there, even over a few days such as during holidays, I know that I can easily enough get my weight back down again within a week or two, and all this without counting calories or food units.

So I think it's certainly worth giving it a try, unless, of course, you personally find it easier to follow and more effective to count calories or food units. Just do what works best for you.

Bite-Size Tip 9

Learn How to Cook Simple Meals for Yourself

Another challenge dieters face is that many diet systems ask you to prepare and cook from scratch a whole menu of calorie-controlled or unit-based meals. Worse still, many of these meals need lots of ingredients, some of which I've never even heard of and wouldn't recognise, and which you have to hunt the shopping aisles to track down.

But the sad fact is that a lot of people don't do much "real" cooking these days, be it of healthy food or not. There are a variety of reasons for this, of course, not least of which is because they can't be bothered to learn how or are simply too bloomin' lazy – or maybe they feel they just don't have the time to go to the hassle of shopping for all the bits and pieces they'll need for a meal, and then set about cooking it. And, of course, many people get home after a long day at work totally tired-out, and the last thing they want to do is spend an hour or so in the kitchen slaving over a chopping board and hot stove cooking some complicated dish that'll take them all of five minutes to eat. These are the sorts of reasons why eating easy and quick-to-prepare things like pasta, oven chips, pizzas and ready meals is so popular.

And I'm not criticising here, by the way – well, not too much, anyway. I'm merely pointing out an easily provable truth that I have been guilty of myself. But the fact remains that if you really do want to lose your excess fat, and keep it off forever, then sooner rather than later you're going to need to adopt healthier eating habits. And, unless you have someone to do all the cooking for you, you're going to have to learn how to cook healthy dishes for yourself, even if only simple ones. If you think that's going to be too much for you, then you obviously don't want to lose weight that much after all, and so you may as well not bother and just stay fat; sorry to be so blunt here, but that's probably the truth of it.

To help get you into the right mindset, start off gently, exploring easy-to-prepare and easy-to-cook healthy meals. It may well spark off a life-long passion for cooking: such things have been known. And there are literally thousands of books and websites out there full of recipes for every taste and dietary need, both simple and complicated. So you have absolutely no excuse on that count. The chances are, you'll even find cookery classes and courses offered at your nearest college. If formal classes don't appeal, maybe you can do as I did, and ask someone you know who is a good cook to teach you – my wife and especially my mother-in-law, a wonderful cook, have been my personal cookery tutors. But I am thinking about going on one or two courses myself, such as baking or bread-making or soup-making. I'm even thinking of heading out to southern Italy for a cooking holiday with one of my lovely aunties-in-law. She happens to be another brilliant cook who prepares a lot of her own sauces, jams, and breads, along with a whole host of Italian dishes, including her own pasta and gnocchi from scratch (I haven't asked her yet but I'm sure she'll be a willing teacher).

I actually enjoyed learning how to cook tasty and healthy meals for myself and my wife, rather than relying on just heating up things like pasta or rice and sauces or some ready-made food, such as pies – which any fool can do – or depending on pre-processed ready meals, however "healthy" they claim to be. And I do find it very satisfying to be able to prepare a delicious and healthy meal from scratch, including, I was surprised to find, chopping vegetables for the pot or pan; it's almost therapeutic. Almost.

What's more, it's not like you have to learn loads of different meals. Just ten or a dozen or so will give you plenty of variety; even half a dozen or fewer well-chosen meals to pick from can do this. In fact, research shows that successful dieters and "weight-maintainers" tend to eat from a pretty limited menu from day-to-day. I've spoken to many successful dieters who, like me, eat exactly the same breakfast every day. For instance, most weeks my wife chooses from about three breakfast options, then from just two or three lunch options, and finally from no more than about eight or ten main meal options. And that's it. Such a pretty limited menu makes life a lot easier too, so it's worth considering.

Incidentally, research – if not common sense – also shows that you're more likely to keep your rate of weight-loss, as well as your final lowest maintainable weight, if you eat more or less about the same calorific amount of food every day, and especially from week to week. I don't count calories myself but I know from experience, as well as from the daily reading on my weight scale, that I tend to eat about the same amount of calories over a period of a few days, even at weekends and on holidays these days. It's just become a habit for me.

But, nonetheless, it's nice to have a bit of a variety in your menu, including meals of varying complexity. When I started to cook properly, I set myself the task of learning to cook at least one new meal every month or so when I was working from home. You can see just how quickly you could build up a nice range of meals to choose from in this way.

Bite-Size Tip 10
Don't Eat Too Much Highly Processed Food

When it comes to pre-processed or what some call "ultra-processed" food products and ready meals, I don't eat many of them myself, apart from the odd soya- and Quorn-based product. Being vegetarian, I obviously don't eat any meat products anyway. Pre-processed and convenience meals are fine to eat in moderation, not only because the meals might be tricky to prepare for the average person, but also for their obvious ease of preparation, especially after a long day's work when you feel just too tired to cook anything from scratch.

But, processed ready meals can prove expensive, especially the "higher-quality" ones with healthier ingredients and few additives, not least because the portion sizes are often not enough for a hungry person, so you have to buy two meals. More importantly, and more worryingly, scientists warn us that most ultra-processed foods can lead to a number of negative health effects, including obesity, if eaten too often.

And the sad fact is that for too many people, especially fat ones, what we might call "real food" has been replaced by things like salty snacks, sugary cereals, industrially-made bread and desserts, ready meals and reconstituted meats, and that's alongside sweetened soft drinks. All these look attractive (and are also attractively packaged), and are designed with sweet or salty tastes that make us want to eat and drink even more. But there is little or even nothing nutritious about many of them.

Ultra-processed foods are basically new creations of the profit-driven food industry. They are made in a factory with industrial ingredients and additives invented by "food scientists", and bear little resemblance to the natural fruit, vegetables, meat or fish used to cook a proper meal at home. They're made with low-cost ingredients that usually have little nutritional quality, not least in terms of the amount of free sugars they contain, as well as sodium (salt) and saturated fat, and they tend to be much lower in proteins, minerals and vitamins. Processed foods also often contain too many potentially unhealthy chemicals, preservatives, flavourings, salt, starch and fat – and goodness only knows what else. They're also usually pretty high in calories too, which is bad news for us dieters.

Worse, highly processed foods can become addictive. And what's even worse still for our health – though not for the profits of the food industry – is that more and more people around the globe are now buying these foods.

For instance, between 1991 and 2008, ultra-processed foods made up a tenth to more than half of the household diet in several European countries (Portugal at 10.2%, the UK at 50.7%). There's no reason to think these figures have gone down since 2008; I'd wager they've got much higher. Interestingly, in most northern European countries – like Austria, Belgium, Germany, Ireland and the UK – these foods made up more than a third of the household diet. Only in parts of what many people regard as the healthier-eating southern European countries – like Portugal, Spain, Italy, Greece, Cyprus and France (probably southern France, I bet) – these arguably more unhealthy foods fall at or below one-fifth (about 20%) of the household diet. A lesson here, somewhere.

So, if you do indulge in processed foods, they are best only eaten now and again, perhaps no more than twice a week. And however often you eat them, they should only make up a small part of your overall meal. Ideally you should eat far more fresh vegetables to give a healthier and more balanced diet.

Bite-Size Tip 11
Snack Between Meals if You Feel the Need

There's nothing intrinsically wrong with snacking between meals, even when you're trying to lose weight. In fact, some people find snacking to be a part of their successful weight-loss plan. Moreover, some people I've spoken to tell me that they find it really hard not to snack between meals, whether they're dieting or not, with one or two people saying that if they don't have a small snack they feel unwell, if not desperately hungry.

Some argue that snacking between meals is healthy because it helps to even out your blood sugar and insulin levels through your waking day, avoiding potentially unhealthy spikes and troughs.

I can take it or leave it when it comes to snacking, not least because I very rarely feel peckish between meals. That said, mainly out of what I regard as a healthy habit rather than being hungry, I tend to eat a small piece or two of fresh fruit with my mid-morning coffee break. In fact, I follow an "early time-restricted feeding" habit (known as eTRF or "intermittent fasting" by some), in which I choose to eat all my food in the first half of my waking day, usually before about 2 pm. I have yet to become aware of any health problems associated with this eating habit or the huge, 16–18 hour gap between my last meal in the early afternoon and breakfast the following morning. On the contrary, the health benefits of adopting such a restricted pattern of eating seem to be compelling for those who can manage it and who have no underlying health conditions which could be aggravated by it.

Either way, the obvious advice about snacking is that it's best to only have healthy foods and avoid things with too much sugar and fat. However, if you are a bit of a chocoholic, cheeseaholic or buiscuitoholic, for instance, then snacking daily on the odd *small* portion of chocolate, cheese or a biscuit or two shouldn't cause too many problems for your weight loss or weight maintenance, as long as you factor it in to your total daily food intake.

Bite-Size Tip 12

Engage in Some *Enjoyable* Regular Exercise as Part of Your Weight-Loss Programme

Scientific evidence shows that, surprising as it may seem, exercise *alone* doesn't make as much difference to people's weight-loss as you might expect; no more than a few pounds across a year for most people. So, most people won't lose much weight relying *just* on exercise; they need to cut back on food as well. It's known as the "exercise paradox" and it's all to do with the way your body and brain compensate when you start burning more energy through physical activity. For example, your body might start using less energy in other ways, like slowing down your metabolism, which means you burn fewer calories. That's why you need to eat a little less even when you engage in regular exercise.

Lots of physical activity can also make you hungrier, which means you eat more if you're not mindful of the fact. This can happen without you even noticing, because you may end up eating only about ten percent more than normal – that's just one extra mouthful for every ten you take. So it can sneakily become a problem if you're *just* using physical exercise to lose weight.

On the other hand, even mildly vigorous exercise early in your day – such as going for a brisk twenty- or thirty-minute walk – can help to keep your metabolism running at a higher rate for longer into your day, which means you burn more calories. Moreover, strength-based exercise such as weight training has been proven to be helpful in weight loss as well, mostly because of the greater amount of energy your bigger muscles then need.

Then there's the newish fad of High Intensity Interval Training, or HIIT, which has been shown in numerous recent small studies to be very good for fatty weight-loss too, not least because it causes you to burn off more calories in a much shorter period of time than, say, jogging or brisk walking. For instance, one study showed that a 20-minute HIIT workout produced the same amount of calorie-burning weight loss as exercising continuously at a moderate intensity for 60 minutes. The HIIT exercises involved do not necessarily require any special equipment, so they can be done at home away from smelly and noisy – and often expensive – gyms full of sweaty people obsessing about themselves in the mirror. HIIT can include such energetic things as jumping jacks, squats, push-ups, step-ups, jumping star-bursts, cycling, running and jogging, running on the spot, and energetic walking; basically all things to get you really puffing and panting, and get your heart pounding. Common ways of doing HIIT involve 20- to 30-second bursts going all out as fast as you can, followed by a few brief minutes of much lower intensity moving about.

Speaking personally, I find HIIT training all a bit too much effort and bother, and I infinitely prefer to go for an invigorating 60-80 minute walk instead, even if it does take three or four times longer to achieve the same amount of calorie burn as HIIT. HIIT physically and emotionally feels too much like exercise to me, where walking doesn't because I enjoy it for its own sake. For me at any rate, regular walking has massively more mental, emotional, physical and wellbeing benefits generally than HIIT training. But it is down to personal preference and choice, and maybe HIIT training will be better for you, so at least consider it.

Either way, nobody can deny the many other health benefits of regular exercise, to your muscles and bones, your cardiovascular and respiratory systems, and even to your brain. So everyone should engage in some form of regular exercise, preferably moderate or brisk, a few times each week. Moderate–brisk exercise would be something like steady swimming up and down a pool, jogging, speed cycling or brisk walking, where your breathing and heart-rate picks up a bit while you're at it. There's also the cosmetic effect of better-toned muscles as a result of all this exercise, which make your body look leaner, fitter and healthier, too, which is an added bonus.

Official guidelines in both the UK and the US say that healthy adults should aim to do at least 150 minutes of moderate or brisk exercise each week – that's only two hours and thirty minutes out of a week. And some research shows that it doesn't seem to matter how you clock-up the two-and-half hours: spreading it evenly across the week or in just one or two big bursts. And if two-and-a-half hours of exercise sounds a lot to cram in to your weekly schedule, one option is to just do a brisk ten-minute walk in the morning, the same again at lunchtime and the same again in the evening, clocking up thirty minutes in total during the day. Done over five days, that would give your total of 150 minutes: job done. Such a schedule shouldn't be too hard to fit into anyone's week. For example, you could walk just part of the way to and from your workplace, and go for a ten-minute walk during your lunch break, which has proven psychological benefits as well. And for those who don't work at all, then they have absolutely no excuse whatsoever for not exercising regularly, the shameful sluggards.

As for those people who claim to be far too busy to devote two-and-a-half hours each week to such moderate–brisk exercise, then they can cut it back to about half that time (one-and-a-quarter hours) if they're happy to do more energetic, vigorous, puffin' and pantin', raise-a-sweat exercise, such as fast swimming, fast cycling, power-walking, running or a game of squash. And, just as with the moderate–brisk exercise, this more vigorous exercise can also be done in bouts as short as ten minutes at a time across a week.

In addition, each week you should also aim to do some muscle-strengthening activities (e.g. press-ups or digging in the garden) on at least two days, along with some regular stretching exercises as well.

I always enjoyed brisk walking myself, but in my fat days I often only went for such tramps three or maybe four times each week, usually for about an hour or so at a time. But wanting to do more, all I did was gradually increase how often I walked, rain or shine, until these days I generally go for a brisk walk at least five times a week, and almost always for well over an hour. And I really do enjoy it too, which is obviously the reason I find it easy to do, requiring zero willpower (a little secret of success I'll discuss elsewhere).

If brisk walking sounds good to you, too – pretty much anyone can do it – then one of the motivational secrets here is to find places where you *really* enjoy walking, preferably locally or somewhere easy to get to, especially if you want to walk several times each week as I do. Since 2003, I've been grateful to be able to choose to live in what, to me, are beautiful parts of the UK amidst some of my favourite landscapes of hills, mountains, forests, lakes and rivers. This was first in the Lake District in Cumbria, north-west England, and now on the edge of the marginally smaller Trossachs National Park in Stirlingshire, central Scotland, which mercifully to me has only a tiny fraction of the tourism as the Lake District does (but don't mention this to too many people, please).

But having spent the first 42 years of my life living in London, I still do really enjoy being a strolling flâneur around interesting and vibrant towns and cities, including central London when I go south, or around nearby Glasgow which is one of my favourite cities, not just because I got to know my wife there. In fact, when I spend a day in great cities like London or Glasgow I frequently end up walking about ten or more miles as I wander about aimlessly – which is what "flâneuring" involves.

What's especially interesting to me is that these days, if I don't get in a regular good walk, it seems a bit strange somehow, and I feel that something's missing from my day, which it is, I suppose. That's the power of habits, which I'll talk much more about later. Also, recently I've started cycling in dry weather, which I am enjoying, too, but when I really don't want to get a soaking on a rainy day I'll sometimes resort to 30 minutes or so on my home elliptical trainer exercise machine, which also gives me a good cardio-vascular workout as well. But I much prefer, and genuinely enjoy, walking and cycling.

Of course, some fat people, especially really enormous ones, find even the mere thought of exercise of any sort totally depressing and exhausting, even simple walking. This is natural and to be expected, as I'll explain elsewhere. But even the fattest person with two functioning legs can walk, even if only very slowly and only for a very short distance. And taking up regular walking, even for just a gentle ten minutes at first, will at least help get a hugely fat person into the mindset of taking regular exercise and moving about generally. The idea is to create a habit, and this can be done by frequent repetition of even short walks.

Another mindset I urge everyone to adopt is to take every chance you can to move around in the course of a day. I'm always looking for ways to use my muscles and so use up physical energy, thereby burning more calories. For example, when I work from home I spend a lot of my time sitting at a desk writing and stuff. So I try to get up and walk about for a few minutes every hour or so, sometimes trotting up and down the stairs two or three times to give my musculoskeletal, cardiovascular and respiratory systems a mini workout. When I have to go up or down to a different floor in buildings such as hotels and offices, I rarely use the lift or escalator – even carrying heavy luggage – but use the stairs if I can manage it. When I drive to the supermarket, or if I need a break on a long motorway journey, I now always automatically park my car at the far end of the car park, which means I have further to walk to get to and from the building. And when I'm using my mobile or cordless phone, I try to stand and walk about while I'm chatting; sometimes I'll even go for a walk into my local hills or have a session on my home elliptical cross-trainer when I'm on a long call.

So look about for opportunities to move about more. For example, if your house has two toilets on separate floors, always use the one on the other floor to where you are. In my case, to make climbing the stairs even more calorie consuming, I wear a massive rucksack full of heavy bricks. Only joking (though not a bad idea in itself, if you think about it).

After doing this so often, I now take chances to move about like this almost without thinking, and the very notion of parking close to the supermarket or taking a lift or escalator up or down one floor absolutely horrifies me. That's the power of habits for you.

FAT FACT
Psychological Benefits of Regular Exercise

Hopefully, by now you're fully convinced of the physical benefits of regular exercise, especially that it helps you to lose weight, and look fit and well toned.

But regular exercise has many psychological benefits too.

For instance, studies have shown the benefits of regular exercise to "brain health". These include improving mental and emotional health and cognitive ability, such as better decision-making, concentration and memory, along with giving a better sense of emotional wellbeing generally.

And it can affect our personality, too. For instance, US research published in April 2018 reported that being more physically active can make people more *extroverted*, *conscientious*, *agreeable* and *open to new experience*. A few of the benefits of these personality changes are:

- extroverted people experience more positive emotions
- higher conscientiousness is linked to more success in life
- being more agreeable means more people will like you, and all that implies

- being open to new experience is linked to increased creativity and intelligence

What's more, the research showed that these changes to personality persist over years. From this same research, it follows that staying a sedentary, lazy sluggard and couch potato is linked to the opposite pattern in personality. So, sedentary people can become more introverted, less conscientious, more disagreeable, and less open to new experience, along with the subsequent negative consequences.

The study's authors also found that a lazy lifestyle can be linked to depression. They said, "it is possible that the long-term functional limitations and depressive symptoms that result from a physically inactive lifestyle may be reflected in a lower tendency to experience positive emotions, be enthusiastic, and be agreeable."

The study concluded that its findings "provide evidence that a physically inactive lifestyle is associated with long-term detrimental personality trajectories". Doesn't sound too encouraging, does it?

But the good news here is that only small amounts of regular exercise like I described are enough, over the years, to lead to the more positive changes to brain health and personality, and the resulting life benefits.

Bite-Size Tip 13
Don't Buy Food You Don't Want to Eat

One of the best bits of advice anyone ever gave me about food shopping was to always eat a bar of chocolate just before you go, as it's actually good for both your wallet and your waistline. Sage advice indeed.

So on that note, here's some quick rules about food shopping I tried to keep to, especially in my early days of dieting when temptations were greatest:

Never go shopping if you feel peckish or hungry. If you do, you're likely to buy more than you need, especially extra snacks and treats. I don't actually suggest you eat a bar of chocolate before you go, as it's rather counterproductive for your weight-loss plan, but I almost always go shopping myself soon after I've eaten my breakfast or lunch.

Make a list of the things you need before you go shopping. Then stick to that shopping list absolutely rigidly, and don't buy any food at all that's *not* on the list. Write your list carefully, because if you find you've forgotten something you need once you get to the shop, hard luck, because you can't buy it if it's not on the list. The *only* exceptions I would allow myself to this rule are:

1. things I'd forgotten to list which I need to actually prepare or cook my food, such as cooking oil, stock cubes, gravy, bread, spreads like jam or butter, and condiments
2. zero or near-zero calorie items like coffee or tea
3. food items I need to buy for someone else, in my case that's just my wife

Shopping lists like this are actually pretty easy for me because I usually eat exactly the same breakfast and fruit with my main meal every day when I'm at home, so the only variables are the items for my main meal itself.

If you have a lot of trouble resisting treats – such as chocolate, sweets, biscuits/cookies, potato chips/crisps, cakes and ice cream

– then simply don't buy them. If they're not within easy reach at home, then you're obviously far less likely to eat them!

If temptation is great, then avoid all shopping aisles that contain the snacks and treats you want too much.

Never buy more food than you need between now and the next time you plan to go food shopping, even if it's food that has a long shelf-life or use-by date, or even which you can easily freeze. The temptation I found here in the early days was that I was more likely to eat more than I needed if I had plenty of food in the house that would last beyond the next time I planned to go shopping. I usually go food shopping about every four days, mostly because I like my fruit fresh.

I do realise these rules are easier to stick to if you're only buying for yourself, and maybe for your partner, too. You may have to be a bit more flexible if you're also buying for young children. That said, only keeping healthy food at home for your kids is no bad thing; you can always buy them treats when you are all out and about.

Bite-Size Tip 14
Celebrate Your Weight-Loss Successes

Losing weight is difficult. At times, it can be *really* difficult, and you will certainly struggle from time to time. Looking at this from a more positive point of view, when you do gradually and consistently lose weight you will have achieved something important. So, consciously acknowledge that achievement. Give yourself due credit and feel justifiable pride at your triumphs. When you consciously feel proud of yourself, it can bolster your self-confidence and make you aware that you're being effective, strong and in control. So make sure you celebrate some of your well-earned successes as you go along your weight-loss journey. You could celebrate by mentally noting that you have passed or reached a stage or weight-loss milestone, or you could give yourself a reward of some kind.

That said, while celebrating and rewarding your achievements, in the early stages especially it can also help to keep mindful of how far you have to go to reach your weight-loss goal, rather than focusing on how far you've come already. This will stop you becoming complacent about your progress and will remind you how far you still have to go. Either way, it's still possible to celebrate a success.

Now, it could be argued that the reward for meeting a weight-loss milestone, including adopting a new healthy habit, is reaching the milestone *itself*, so just acknowledging this success psychologically should be enough. It's much the same as saying that the reward for a job well done is the accomplishment of the job itself. This was my own strategy, and it worked really well for me, so I highly recommend it. But some people do better if they reward themselves something tangible, not just a psychological pat on the back. If for no other reason, this is because the reward is something to look forward to, which can itself be an effective motivation. Moreover, such a reward can sometimes give a greater sense of achievement than just a mental celebration. So you need to find out what works best for you. Just note that I talk a lot more about motivation elsewhere, so look it up.

Either way, the most obvious things to celebrate are stages of weight-loss goals as you go along. For instance, I suggest aiming to lose no more than between half-a-pound to one pound (0.2 to 0.45 kilos) of fatty weight each week on average for a healthy, sustainable and easier-to-achieve target. Doing the maths (or the "math" if you're from the US), that works out at losing between about two pounds and four pounds (0.9 to 1.8 kilos) each month. It should be easier to lose half-a-pound each week than to lose one pound, which will make your whole weight-loss experience far more tolerable and, ideally, even enjoyable. So, let's say that you're happy to plod along at this easy, low rate of weight-loss of about half-a-pound each week on average, or about two pounds each month. Then why not celebrate every time you lose at least two pounds of fat each month?

Or, you might prefer to celebrate every time you lose, say, two or three pounds, regardless of how long it took you. But, don't celebrate too often: these are meant to be special events, so I suggest rewarding yourself no more than about once a month. And obviously you'll want a really big celebration, and maybe even an impressive reward too, once you reach your ultimate weight-loss target. You should also think about celebrating at times after that if you manage to stick to your new healthier weight, which itself can be a challenge.

You should pat yourself on the back when you make behavioural changes that help you lose weight, not just when you reach a certain number on the scales. For example, you could reward yourself if you managed to meet a goal of moderate to brisk exercise on, say, every other day, or about fifteen times each month, achieving the minimum 150 minutes of exercise each week recommended for most adults. All successful changes in behaviour deserve some appreciation.

If you do want to celebrate with a tangible or "measurable" reward, then make sure to pick an appropriate one. It should *not* conflict with your desired outcome, so I do not advise giving yourself food treats, for obvious reasons, I hope. That said, some people do reward themselves with a "rest day" from their successful dieting once every week or two, perhaps indulging, or overindulging, in their favourite fatty or sugary foods or treats by eating pretty much whatever they fancy on that particular day. Such a day is sometimes called a "cheat day". That's your choice, of course, but it pays to be careful with food rewards, especially if there's a risk that it might badly impact your weight-loss plans.

I'd also suggest that you avoid buying yourself expensive rewards that you can't really afford. That said, I think it is okay to splash out on something extravagant when you reach your final weight-loss target, though not so expensive that it will get you into debt, of course.

Either way, and caveats aside, you need to choose a reward that's valuable enough to you *personally*; one that really does feel like a proportionate reward for what you've achieved; even something small can be effective. So maybe *don't* buy yourself a new car or a new house or a world cruise just because you've managed to lose a few pounds of weight in a month or two. Though I suppose such a lavish reward might be worth considering once you've managed to reach your final target weight and maintained it for at least a year or two; and if you can afford it, of course.

But such particularly extravagant rewards aside, here's a few tangible reward suggestions you might like to consider, based on conversations I've had with people over the years:

- Buy yourself "something nice" with the money you've saved from not buying all those fatty things such as cakes, chocolate and large caffè lattes
- Spend time in front of the TV watching that box-set you've been meaning to plough through, or curled-up with that book you've been meaning to read
- Have a massage or a spa session
- Have a traditional wet-shave at a trusted barber (men only, I hope)
- Go to the theatre or to a concert in the best seat you can afford
- Take a day-trip or a weekend away
- Buy a new gadget, such as a new music player, headphones, TV or e-book reader

- Buy a food-processing gadget to make it easier to prepare your healthy meals
- Buy some exercise equipment that you *know* you'll want to use
- Buy a new piece of clothing in a smaller size

And after you've finally reached your target weight *and* managed to maintain it for at least one year, maybe consider:

- A whole new wardrobe of clothes in your new smaller size (don't forget to give away the bigger-size clothes – you'll need the wardrobe-space anyway)
- A holiday where you can show-off your slimmer and fitter-looking body

You'll notice that each of the things I've listed is all about giving you a pleasurable experience of some kind. Studies show that such experience-based rewards are best for making you feel happy. I'm sure you can think of other such things that you would enjoy.

Also, don't forget to share your weight-loss successes with other people: your partner, friends and relatives, and include social media or a weight-loss website with community pages, which are great places to get support and encouragement. Praise for your achievements from other people, especially from those you care about and respect, is rich reward in itself.

Lastly, don't become fixated on working for the reward itself. Because they give you something to aim for and look forward to, these rewards may well help to motivate you to keep going when you're finding it a bit of a struggle and so are not enjoying it, especially in the early days. But I would urge you rather to adopt the mindset that the reward for reaching a milestone, or adopting a new healthy habit, is reaching the milestone or the new habit itself; so just being glad about that can be enough. This won't be a problem if you can design a healthy lifestyle, helping you lose weight, that you find enjoyable and satisfying mentally, emotionally and physically: your new healthier lifestyle is the reward.

Bite-Size Tip 15

Consider Taking a "Cheat Day" Off From Your Diet Now and Again

A popular option of some weight-loss plans is to allow yourself a "cheat day" from time to time, which is one day per week on which you can eat anything and everything you want, no holds barred. In some such plans, you're told to write a list during the week of all the foods you craved so you can enjoy them all at once as a big fat treat on your cheat day. It's not a bad strategy in itself, the thinking being that if you're sticking with your weight-loss plan on six out of seven days, then taking just one day off a week to eat anything you like won't make much of a difference in the long run. That is true to a point, though some people I can think of could easily pack away two or three or even more days' worth of calories in a single day with no problem at all, especially if they're "emotionally" eating, which would obviously do their weight-loss plans no favours at all.

In fact, you'll note that I mentioned something about such cheat days under the last tip, Celebrate Your Weight-Loss Successes, where you might decide to reward yourself with a rest day (a.k.a. cheat day) from your successful dieting once every week or two.

I used this reward day or cheat day strategy myself in the early days of my weight-loss adventure, usually on a Saturday, and I did enjoy it, at least at first. But as the weeks went on I began to feel less and less inclined to pig-out and eat myself sick once a week. In fact, I soon began to feel unpleasantly stuffed on such days of gluttony —eating to excess because I *could* rather than because I was actually hungry – and I would also feel guilty afterwards, regretting that I'd eaten so much for no good reason. I came to realise that indulging like this felt much worse than sticking with my diet. And this was even though I knew that I wasn't eating so much in a single day that it would significantly slow down my weight-loss in the long-term. In the end, I just stopped enjoying cheat days and, because I didn't need or want them anymore, I didn't bother with them at all after a while. I suspect that once I'd realised – even unconsciously at first – that indulging to excess on a given day was actually worse than sticking with my diet, the urge to indulge lost its appeal. Instead, I actually began to feel real pleasure and satisfaction with my self-control in not taking a regular cheat day, not least because I realised that giving into the temptation would become a painful regret rather than give me pleasure.

Perhaps it's enough for me now to know that I can still choose to have cheat days if I want to, and that might well prove true for you, too, if not now, then later. These days, since reaching my maintainable healthy weight, if I fancy eating something fatty or sugary on any day at all, I just have it, be it something like a big pizza, a big bar of chocolate, a large bowl of ice cream (or two), or a big wedge of cheese with biscuits. The key is to eat sensibly and healthily *over time*, such as over a few days or a week or so, enjoying indulgent treats from time to time as part of your normal and generally healthy eating plan.

So, in summary, certainly think about taking a cheat day off from your diet now and again, especially in the early weeks of your weight-loss plans, but you may well discover after a while, as I did, that you really don't need to or even want to have such a regular day off.

Bite-Size Tip 16
Accept That You May End Up as a Thin Fat Person

I read somewhere (can't remember where) that most ex-alcoholics are actually alcoholics who don't drink any more. Similarly, I read somewhere else (can't remember where either) that ex-smokers, particularly those who were chronically heavy smokers, are smokers who don't smoke any more. In other words, I gather that ex-alcoholics and ex-smokers still do feel the urge to indulge from time to time, but have successfully learned to manage their urge, even if they only feel that urge now and again. Put another way, it's not that they won't still feel the need to drink alcohol or smoke cigarettes from time to time, especially in the early days, but they are able to stop themselves from indulging at all. From conversations I've had with the odd ex-alcoholic and ex-smoker, this does seem to be true for many such people.

The important point I want to make here is that the *temptation* to indulge in the former habit or addiction is still lurking in the background, waiting to pounce and strike if they don't maintain their vigilance. So that's why many ex-alcoholics are alcoholics who don't drink any more, and ex-smokers are smokers who don't smoke any more. It's also why relapse is common, especially amongst alcoholics, many of whom are never really able to break the iron grip of alcohol on their lives, sad to say.

From my research, I would argue that all this is probably true for most of our deeply ingrained and long-term, unhelpful habitual thoughts, emotions and behaviours, including those to do with eating patterns. You need to accept that it may well be the case that you'll never be able to totally rid yourself of such unhelpful ideas. More likely, the best you'll be able to do is learn to manage them in some way, such as by weakening them by overwriting and overwhelming them with more helpful habits of thinking, feeling and behaving, instead. And just as with ex-alcoholics and ex-smokers, you'll probably need to stay alert to make sure your old unhelpful attitudes don't leap out and reassert themselves given half the chance. The sad fact is that deep-rooted habits and addictions of any sort, be they mental, emotional, or physical – including eating addictions – are never easily shed, if at all; they were probably years in the making and might well take years in the breaking.

So if all this surmising of mine is true, then if you've been fat for a long time, and even if you've managed to slim down to reach your target weight and maintain it for a while, you may still have to accept that you're now a *thin fat person*, with the threat of relapse back to your old, unhealthy eating habits never far away. I know this to be true from my own personal experience, after successful weight-loss and healthy weight maintenance these last few years. Thus far, I know I'd find it easy enough to overindulge in fatty and sugary foods if I allowed myself to; the temptation is still there, lurking in the background. I keep myself vigilant with my healthy eating and exercise habits, not least by not getting complacent – I remind myself that the rate of relapse for dieters is extremely high: the overwhelming majority pile the fat back on again sooner or later, often getting even fatter, even after years of staying slim.

Bite-Size Tip 17

Enrich and Enhance Your Life in Different Ways to Be Happy

It's a sad fact that many people eat too much – and so are fat and unhealthy as a result – because they're not happy. At some level, they're just not as content and fulfilled as they could be. This is usually because they're not meeting one or more of their fundamental human needs and, probably because of this, have a low sense of self-worth; both things I discuss at length elsewhere. More often than not, such fat people are usually emotional eaters, who comfort-eat to make themselves feel better about their lives, even without realising it.

By the way, I talk a lot more about emotional eating in Part 3 of my Diet Tricks guide, *Why You Eat the Way You Do* (see in particular the sections "What Sort of Eater Are You?" and "There Are Two Sorts of Hunger: Metabolic and Hedonic"). You can find these on the DietTricks.com website. I strongly suggest that you learn about these things, not least because they can help you understand why you eat the way you do and what you can do about it.

It's worth quoting here the poignant, insightful and still painfully relevant observation of Henry David Thoreau in his nineteenth-century literary classic *Walden*, in which he writes the sobering words: "The mass of men lead lives of quiet desperation. What is called resignation is confirmed desperation ... A stereotyped but unconscious despair is concealed even under what are called the games and amusements of mankind." And I'm pretty sure he'd include "womankind" here too if he was writing nowadays.

So thinking of your weight-loss efforts, you can learn to become happier with your weight, whatever it is, as well as happier about the healthier lifestyle choices and habits you take on board to help you lose weight, by focusing on exploring ways of enriching and enhancing your life more generally. Explore ways of enriching things like your relationships (with partner, relatives, friends and colleagues), your home life, your recreational life, your job, if and how you measurably contribute to society in some way (such as via charitable contribution of some sort), your spirituality or religious expression, and your overall emotional, mental and physical health generally. I recommend that you should also aim to explore and fulfill what you see as your "meaning" and "purpose" in life.

To live a happier life generally, I would also urge you to live "authentically" and with integrity according to your own core beliefs and values – rather than other people's or society's. Strive to *be*, to *do* and to *have* all the things you really want and *need* in your life, especially the things you might have been shying away from and putting off until you lose weight. Aim to *want what you have*, rather than *have what you want*. The overall aim of all this is to live a happy and flourishing life: content, satisfied and fulfilled with who you *are*, what you *do* and what you *have*, day-by-day.

To finish here, if you feel that you are flourishing in all aspects of life, and have made your life richer, more fulfilled and happier, then it is not so likely that you'll focus on your weight, whatever it is. You'll be more likely to be *happy enough* with whatever weight-loss you are able to achieve and maintain in the long-term, even if it isn't as much as you'd initially hoped. It worked for me, so give it a go.

Bite-Size Tip 18

Accept that You May Only Be Able to Lose Ten Percent of Your Weight

It's important to accept the fact that, according to research, you're probably going to be able to *most easily* achieve and maintain *only* about a ten percent weight loss, and perhaps even less. It's important to accept this because I don't want you to start off with unrealistic expectations, which might result in crushing disappointment. I'm not saying that you *definitely* won't be able to lose more weight than this, especially if you're really fat and obese, but what I am saying is that to do so will almost definitely require a lot more constant effort from you to achieve and, most importantly, to maintain than losing only about ten percent or so. I would add that you will find this all significantly easier to do if you embrace as many of the weight-loss tips in this book as you can, and consider learning about even more on my associated website.

For example, if you have a current starting weight of, say, 12 stone and 12 pounds (or 180 pounds/81.6 kilos), then you can reasonably hope to be able to lose up to about 1 stone and 4 pounds of fat (about 18 pounds/8.16 kilos) without too much problem, especially if you follow much of my advice. This means that you can hope to reach and keep a stable weight, *in the long-term*, of about 11 stone and 8 pounds (about 162 pounds/73.4 kilos) without too much of a problem. I know this to be true from personal experience, as these are my own weight numbers: the example is my own.

As I said a moment ago, this is not to say you won't be able to lose more than ten percent of your current weight. You most certainly can if you have enough willpower and motivation, and can establish some strong lifestyle habits – things I talk about at some length elsewhere, including how to strengthen them, so look it up. It's rather that, for most people, losing more than about ten percent of their weight is just not easy to stick at long-term, with most people ending up feeling too deprived of enjoyable food and/or expected to do too much physical exercise. It's the difference between being able to reach and sustain long-term what's known as your lowest *achievable* weight versus your lowest *maintainable* weight; things I also talk about in more detail elsewhere. But for now, your lowest *achievable* weight is, as the name implies, the lowest weight you will be able to achieve with your best weight-loss efforts. Your lowest *maintainable* weight is, as it implies, the lowest weight you will be able to keep to most easily over time, and is always higher than your lowest achievable weight, which is harder to maintain.

In my case, I found that by using the tools and techniques I'm sharing with you, I was able to reach a lowest achievable weight of 11 stone (154 pounds/69.8 kilos) within a year or so without too much difficulty. But over time I realised that staying at this lowest weight I could reach was just too much for me; it needed more energy, effort and sacrifices than I was prepared to make in the long-term. So, I relaxed things to indulge in some more agreeable eating and exercise habits until I reached a balance that I enjoyed enough to be able to maintain long-term. With this, my weight crept up again until it settled at about 11 stone and 8 pounds. This turned out to be about ten percent less than the weight I started off at – totally in line with the scientific studies and theories.

Such studies have shown this maximum weight loss of about ten percent (or even less) is true for most dieters, even those who start off in the obese weight range. I don't want to go into the reasons why right now, beyond saying that the brain seems to have a "fat thermostat set point" and "fat regulating mechanism" which tries to keep the levels of fat stored in the body within a limited range. This is a bit like the thermostat on a central heating system which helps to keep the temperature indoors within a certain limited range. Your fat regulating mechanism works by playing around with things like your metabolic rate, your desire for physical activity and your hunger signals.

Incidentally, if you'd like to learn more about the so-called fat thermostat set point and fat regulating mechanism, and what you can do to counteract or even possibly change them to work in your favour, I go into it in a lot more detail on my website and in Book

3: *Why You Eat the Way You Do*, (see the section "About Ten Percent Weight Loss May Be Your Limit: Your Fat Thermostat").

Either way, just keep in mind that you may not be able to *easily* achieve and maintain as much weight-loss in the long term as you might want.

Bite-Size Tip 19

Remind Yourself Daily Precisely Why You Want to Lose Weight

You're far more likely to be successful if you first think about and write down as many compelling, motivating reasons as you can for *why* you want to lose weight in the first place. You need to clarify and establish precisely what all the consequences are and, perhaps more importantly, all the benefits of losing weight for *you*. You also need to plan for all the obstacles, challenges, barriers and temptations you'll need to overcome along the way to reaching your weight-loss goals.

I go into all the whys and wherefores about doing this in much more detail elsewhere; so do look it up, as I would argue that setting out the *precise, compelling* reasons for why you want to lose weight, and planning for the problems you will meet, are some of the best things you can do to help you to succeed.

It follows that you'll be all the more successful if you constantly remind yourself, every day, of all your reasons for wanting, nay, *needing*, to lose weight. I would also suggest, for extra benefit, that you remind yourself too of how you plan to overcome the difficulties you will probably meet.

This reminder technique is especially useful for days when, for one reason or another, you suspect that you're going to find it particularly hard to stick to your diet. It's also great to use on the spot when you get caught-out unawares, so to speak – when you unexpectedly meet temptations or cravings you find hard to resist. Going through all your reasons for wanting to lose weight can really help at these times, and can save the day. So don't forget them.

Bite-Size Tip 20
Persistence and Determination Can Rewire Your Brain

Last but by no means least, as the well-known cliché goes, you must commit to working towards your weight-loss goals all the time with enthusiastic, persistent and determined intentions and actions. And never, ever put off until tomorrow what you can do today; do it now. "It's the job that's never started as takes longest to finish," as Sam Gamgee's gaffer reportedly says in J. R. R. Tolkien's *The Lord of the Rings*. Also, never, ever give up on an *achievable* and *important* weight-loss goal. Do whatever it takes to succeed; your life may literally depend upon it.

You need to practice, practice and, for good measure, practice even more to rid yourself of unhealthy lifestyle habits and adopt healthier new ones in their place. You need to do this if you want to change your brain in the long-term – to get it to physically re-wire itself. So you need to practice, practice and practice some more all the tools and tips you're going to learn from me, bringing in your emotions while you do so, and, of course, you need to avoid any negative practices like the plague.

Always, always remember:

Nothing in the world can take the place of Persistence.
Talent will not; nothing is more common than unsuccessful
     men with talent
Genius will not; unrewarded genius is almost a proverb
Education will not; the world is full of educated derelicts
Persistence and determination alone are omnipotent
The slogan "Press On" has solved and always will solve the
     problems of the human race.

Calvin Coolidge (1872–1933)
30th president of the USA

Topic 1:
Losing Weight Has
to Matter a Lot to You

Bite-Size Tip 21

Keep an Accurate Record of Everything

Your unconscious mind needs to absorb the fact that losing weight really matters a lot to you. One way of telling it this is to record absolutely *everything* about your weight-loss efforts, in as much detail as possible. This activity all by itself sends a clear and strong message to your mind that losing weight is important to you. So get yourself some form of weight-loss journal.

Moreover, studies show you're more likely to achieve a goal if you keep an accurate record. So make a detailed written account of all your slimming endeavours, including all your really good reasons for desperately wanting to lose weight, your *specific* target weight and date; the *specific* actions you take to slim down as you go along; the obstacles, barriers and temptations you have to overcome and how; along with your daily, weekly and monthly progress generally; and, at least in the early stages, a detailed food and drink diary of your precise daily consumption. You'll get ideas about other things worth writing down in later sections.

Studies also show that you're even more likely to achieve your goal if you send a copy of all your records to a supportive, trustworthy and non-judgmental friend. I say more later on your choice of friend for this purpose.

Write by hand in a notebook or on pages in a ring-binder folder. Studies show that writing by hand, at least initially, can be good for creative thinking – you can always edit what you've written and put it on a computer later if you're more of a rabid anti-Luddite who thinks that writing by hand and books are long dead – or should be.

Use illustrations – the brain likes to think in pictures, so include lots of images, diagrams, tables and graphs. For much the same reason as writing by hand, it's a good idea to do as many of the illustrations yourself where you can – they just need to be good enough for *you* to understand what they represent.

Use lots of colour – different colours in your writings and drawings will make things look more eye-catching, interesting and engaging to your brain.

Choose an inspiring title – think up a snappy title for your "getting slim" magnum opus records – preferably one that makes you smile, and keeps you motivated when you read or think about it.

Bite-Size Tip 22

You Need to Really Want to Lose Weight Badly Enough

You'll find it significantly easier to lose weight if you have some really strong, compelling and emotionally-loaded *personal* reasons for doing so. To get some clarity about your reasons, you could start by writing in your slimming journal a prompting sentence like:

"Getting slim REALLY matters to me because …"
    or
"I really badly want to lose weight because … "

… in both cases listing as many reasons you can think of; the more the merrier.

To help you a little more, here are some questions to ask yourself to see if you really do want to lose weight badly enough:

Why is getting slim absolutely critical to me?
Why do I want to get slim?
How badly do I really want to get slim?
Will getting slim really be enough?
Am I really willing to do whatever it takes?
Am I ready *right now* to put everything on the line and
    do whatever it takes?
Do I believe I can get slim?
Why aren't I slim now?
When I dieted before and failed, why?
Do I have enough passion and desire to get slim?
Is there enough urgency behind my actions?
What do I have to lose by getting slim?
What are all the advantages and benefits that I – and other people
    around me – experience from me getting slim and healthy?
What are all the disadvantages and drawbacks that I – and
    other people around me – experience from me being fat and
    unhealthy?

FAT FACT
Can You Be Fat *and* Fit?

It really depends on what you mean by "fit".

If you're fat, and your question is something like: "Can I still be 'fit' by doing regular physical exercise such as brisk walking, running, cycling, swimming or going to the gym to puff and pant?" – then the answer is almost certainly "yes".

But the scientific research about this question looks at "fitness" in a different way, basically, about your chances of avoiding an early death. It's like this: if you are overweight, are you more likely to die from certain conditions or diseases than if you were not overweight?

Now, some studies show that overweight and obese people have pretty much the same chance of surviving various chronic, fat-related conditions and diseases – such as cardiovascular disease, stroke or diabetes – as healthy-weight people do. Moreover, overweight or obese people who are in other ways physically and "metabolically healthy" have a significantly better chance of surviving those conditions than overweight people who are not as "healthy" and "fit".

What they mean by "metabolically healthy" is that you have only one or two of the following conditions:

- high blood pressure
- high triglycerides (allegedly "bad" cholesterol)
- low high density lipids (HDL or allegedly "good" cholesterol)
- high blood sugar
- high waist circumference (a.k.a. lots of belly fat)

Obviously, the fewer of these conditions you have, the more metabolically healthy you are. Less than one would be ideal!

More specifically, if you're overweight or obese, then your risk of dying of a weight-related condition or disease is about the same as a healthy-weight person, but only if you adopt one or more of the same four healthy lifestyle habits as healthy-weight people do:

1. Eating five or more servings of fruits and vegetables daily (hope springs ever eternal ...)
2. Drinking alcohol in moderation. That's up to one drink per day for women and up to two drinks per day for men (sexist or what)
3. Not smoking (so try not to set yourself on fire, either)
4. Exercising at least three or four times each week, for a total time of at least 150 minutes (yeah, right ... like most people do). There's a wide range of activities that count as exercise, including brisk walking, jogging or running, riding a bicycle or exercise bike, swimming, aerobic exercise, dancing, calisthenics, vigorous garden or yard work, weightlifting, or any other similar moderate to vigorous activities that get you puffing and panting (and for some people gasping for an alcoholic drink or cigarette or both when they collapse in an exhausted heap by the end of it).

In fact, according to the same research, for anyone – whatever their weight – who adopts all four of these healthy habits, their fatty weight seems to make very little difference at all to their survival chances, thus supporting the "fat but fit" claim.

That said, another study found that obese people have a higher chance of suffering from heart disease, stroke or heart failure than overweight or normal-weight people, whether it kills them or not. They have an even higher chance if they are metabolically unfit as well, which includes having high blood pressure, diabetes, abnormal blood fats – such as high "bad" cholesterol levels – and a big, fat belly. Similarly, other studies have concluded that overweight and obese people have higher coronary heart disease risk than lean, average-weight people, even more so if they are metabolically unfit as well. So these last few bits of research challenge the concept of "fit and fat", at least in some respects.

In summary, I think it's fair to say that the fatter you are, then the more chance you have of getting fat-related conditions such as heart disease, heart attack, stroke, diabetes, high blood pressure – and even Alzheimer's and dementia, it seems.

On the other hand, even if you are fat, if you are metabolically healthy and if you keep regular healthy lifestyle habits, then it is less likely that those horrible, fat-related conditions will actually kill you stone dead. That all said, it is now known that there are a dozen or more different types of cancer directly linked to being too fat, and I don't know any scientific evidence that says you're more likely to survive those if you're fat and fit.

Arguably, when all's said and done, it would be much wiser not taking the chance of getting any fat-related conditions or diseases at all in the first place. They would be unpleasant enough, at the very least reducing your quality of life one way or another, and may still end up killing you in the end, however unlikely that is according to the research. There's always some who die in the studies, and it might be you. And the only way you're going to avoid all that unpleasantness and possible early and even agonising death is by not being fat in the first place. It's simple common sense. The choice is yours.

Bite-Size Tip 23

Make Sure You Want to Get Slim for the *Right Personal Reasons*

The benefits of losing weight must really matter to *you* on a deep, *personal* level. You'll find it much harder, if not impossible, if you're trying to slim down just because other people or circumstances say that you should, but deep down you don't really agree with them. To help identify your deep, personal reason or reasons for losing weight you could start by writing in your weight-loss journal a prompting sentence something like:

"Getting slim REALLY matters to me personally because …"

List as many reasons you can think of, though there may only be one.

Bite-Size Tip 24

Make Sure Losing Weight Meets Your Fundamental Human Needs

We all have various fundamental human needs of "being", "doing", "having" and "interacting" in our lives, whether we recognise them or not. Psychologists generally agree that these needs must be met one way or another if you want to live a healthy, fulfilling, contented and flourishing life. Your fundamental human needs include the need for:

- a sense of high self-esteem
- positive emotions most of the time
- a sense of self-efficacy and accomplishment
- resilience in the face of life's challenges
- physical, mental and emotional vitality
- self-determination or autonomy and control
- the ability to work towards worthy and achievable life goals
- a sense of meaning and purpose in life
- a sense of engagement with your job of work

You also have a number of social-emotional needs, such as the need for:

- positive relationships
- acceptance
- attention
- admiration
- affection
- love
- a sense of contribution
- social connection and belongingness

Putting it bluntly, being fat can hinder your ability to meet or satisfy one or more of your fundamental needs in some way, just as losing enough weight can help you to meet and satisfy one or more of them in some way as well. Because you are motivated to act by these needs, whether you are consciously aware of it or not, you are more likely to succeed in slimming down if being slimmer meets one or more of your needs, the more the better.

To help see how losing weight might help you to meet one or more of your fundamental human needs, you could start by writing in your slimming journal a list of the needs, and then answer the following two interrelated questions for each need:

Does being fat hinder me meeting or satisfying this particular fundamental need one way or another, and, if so, how?

How would losing enough weight and slimming down help me to meet and satisfy this need one way or another?

This final little "needs" activity feeds into another action I strongly recommend, under the next tip of "List All the Consequences of Losing Weight and Being Slim, Both to You and to Other People", in which I encourage you to make a list of all the negative results of staying fat and all the positive results of losing weight. Well worth doing both activities, I would say.

Bite-Size Tip 25

List All the Consequences of Losing Weight and Being Slim, Both to You and to Other People

To help convince your mind that losing weight really is important, you need to identify the negative and positive consequences to you and other people of staying fat or losing weight. Sort them into order of their importance to you, then list them in your slimming journal along the lines of:

> *"The specific negative consequences, costs, disadvantages and drawbacks that I personally experience now and will in the future from me staying fat and unhealthy are as follows ...*

And then,

> *"The specific negative consequences, costs, disadvantages and drawbacks that other significant people around me experience now and will in the future from me staying fat and unhealthy are as follows ..."*

Followed by:

> *"The specific positive consequences, benefits and value that I will personally get from losing weight and being slim and healthy are as follows ..."*

And then,

> *"The specific positive consequences, benefits and value that other significant people around me will experience from me losing weight and being slim and healthy are as follows ..."*

Bite-Size Tip 26

Identify Your *True Reason* for Wanting to Lose Weight

Closely related to wanting to lose weight for the right personal reasons and meeting your fundamental human needs, to be truly happy with your slimming efforts you need to establish precisely why you *really truly* do want to lose weight and get slim, at the deepest possible level. You need to ask yourself the question: what will losing weight ultimately do for you? What deep, fundamental human need will losing weight fulfill? To help identify your true reason for wanting to lose weight, you could start by writing in your slimming journal something like:

"The true, deep reason I want to get slim is because …"

Use the "Downward Arrow Technique" to Help Discover Your *True Reasons*

Identifying your true, deep-rooted reasons for wanting to lose weight is vitally important to your success. But such motivating reasons will be bound up in the deep-rooted beliefs and values you hold about yourself, about other people, and about the wider world around you, and how each one of these three areas of your life interact and influence each other.

Even if you think you have identified your true personal reasons for wanting to lose weight already from earlier activities, the "Downward Arrow Technique" can work really well at digging down to your deeper meanings, beliefs and values. So it can reveal deeper motivating reasons and drives, which are usually linked with the need to fulfill particular fundamental human needs.

The basic Downward Arrow Technique is to take one of your reasons for wanting to lose weight you've identified so far, and then ask yourself a series of open questions about it, aiming to discover what deeper meanings lie beneath it. An open question is one which can't be answered with a simple "yes", "no", "maybe" or some particular fact, but rather instead requires a longer answer from you, an answer which requires you to think and reflect more deeply, exposing to yourself your underlying beliefs, values, assumptions, biases, prejudices, opinions and emotions. You've probably unknowingly used such open questions about your weight-loss already, such as, *"Why do I want to lose weight?"*, *"What other benefits will I get from slimming down?"* and *"How do I currently plan to go about shedding the pounds?"*

So, to use the Downward Arrow Technique, you start off by writing down what you currently consider to be your most important, true reason for wanting to lose weight. Then ask yourself a series of open questions intended to explore your thoughts and beliefs behind it. Each time you reveal a deeper underlying belief or idea, you ask yourself another open question about that one.

For example, a good, general open question you could use again and again at each step would be something like, *"Why is that really important to me?"* Once you've thought out the answer to that open question, you could start writing your answer along the lines of: *"It's really important to me because ..."* You can then ask the same *"Why is that really important to me?"* open question about your last answer. With each subsequent answer, you simply keep going "down" with further probing open questions until you reach a belief or idea about yourself, other people, or the world around you that doesn't seem to change any further when you ask any more open questions about it. At this point you will have likely reached the deepest, *core belief* underlying that particular reason for losing weight which you started off with. You can then rephrase this final core belief into a reason that will keep you motivated in your weight-loss efforts.

You don't need to ask the same open question at each step, not least because it might not be relevant. Other useful open questions include: *"What would that mean to me?"*, *"How would it make me feel?"*, *"What else might that achieve for me?"*, *"Suppose that was true, why should it bother me?"*, *"What would be so bad about that?"*, *"What would be the worst possible thing about that?"* or *"What would it say about my future?*" In fact, it might be worth asking two or three of these slightly different open questions at each step just to help give you the best chance of uncovering what might lie beneath.

Using the Downward Arrow Technique might sound like a lot of effort, but it really is worth it. It's a powerful technique, and you'll probably only have to do it once anyway.

Bite-Size Tip 27
Expect to Make Long-Term Lifestyle Changes

If you have been fat for a long time, and assuming it's nothing to do with your "bad genes", it is because of the unhealthy eating and exercise habits you have had until now. It follows that to lose weight and get slim – and, most importantly, stay slim – you will need to change your habits. The best way to think about this is that you will be embracing healthy lifestyle changes and habits. These changes in how you eat and exercise will be long-term, from now on for the rest of your life. This is no bad thing in itself for your overall physical, mental and emotional health.

To help identify the sort of habits you will need to change and adopt as soon as possible, you could start by writing in your slimming journal something like:

> *"To help me lose weight and stay slim for the rest of my life I will need to adopt the following long-term eating and exercise lifestyle habit changes …"*

Bite-Size Tip 28

Expect to Struggle – But Prepare to Beat It

"Hope for the best, but plan for the worst." It's best to assume that you will, at times, struggle and fail to overcome obstacles, setbacks and other temptations as you strive to lose weight and get slim. You just need to have ready a box of cognitive and behavioural tricks that you can use to beat them. You will benefit by just accepting the failure. Try to see the funny side of it if you can, and, most importantly, look for the positives in the experience, especially anything that you can learn from your so-called "mistake". Later on, I write more on the sorts of cognitive and behavioural tools and tricks you can use to overcome obstacles, but in the meantime you could start by writing in your weight-loss journal something like the following pledge to yourself:

> *"I know that losing weight and getting slim will be challenging at times, and so I will expect the inevitable obstacles and setbacks, and deal with them as best I can. When they occur, I will at the very least just accept them as having happened, strive to see the funny side, and look for the positives in the experience, especially what I can learn from the mistake."*

And make sure you mean it.

Bite-Size Tip 29

Be Kind and Compassionate to Yourself About Your Body

Remember that you are only a less-than-perfect human being. So, strive hard to just accept your body despite what you think others may see as imperfections – fat, warts, and all. Develop a more positive body image.

Being kinder and more compassionate towards yourself in this way will reduce your concerns about weight and body shape, and help you cope better with everyday setbacks and personal disappointments as well – be they diet-related or otherwise.

To help you learn to accept yourself in these ways, you could write in your weight-loss journal something like the following pledge:

> *"I will at all times strive hard to be kind and compassionate towards myself, warts and all, accepting my body as it is, regardless of what other people may think of me."*

And, again, make sure you mean it.

Bite-Size Tip 30

Don't Look to Lose Weight to Make You Feel Happier With Your Life Generally

Many fat and obese people have the understandable notion that losing weight and getting slim will inevitably make them feel much happier about themselves. And it often does, at least in some ways. But don't bet on it, especially if you decide *not* to follow much of the other guidance and advice I offer you in this programme after all; following even just a few of the tools and tips I describe can make all the difference here.

But being *generally* contented, satisfied, fulfilled and flourishing in life (a.k.a. "happy") is a many-faceted aspect of your life. No single thing will bring you significant overall happiness, not even losing weight and getting slim.

Topic 2:
What Is Your
Weight-Loss Goal?

Bite-Size Tip 31

Make Your Weight-Loss Goal Positive and Result-Oriented

Studies show that it generally works best if you think about and write down your weight-loss plans in positive terms of what you *will* be, *will* feel, *will* do and *will* have, rather than in negative terms of what you won't be, feel, do or have. So, if you can make your slimming goal positive and result-oriented, that will help keep your mind focused in an emotionally positive way on what you're moving towards and aiming to achieve.

Of course, if all that positive thinking fails, you can always try thinking about things in more negative terms of what it's like to be fat, such as the psychological and physical pain and hassle you're trying to move away from.

In fact, some people do find it works to think of all the negative stuff first, and what they're striving to move away from by losing weight, and then, when they're feeling thoroughly miserable and depressed, switch their focus to all the positive stuff instead, and then keep their focus as best they can on that.

What approach works best is probably a personality thing, affected by genes, upbringing, and societal and cultural influences.

Bite-Size Tip 32
Be Clear About Your Weight-Loss Goal

You need to write down precisely how much weight you initially want to lose, and when. For the best chance of success, this first slimming goal needs to be *SMART*: *Specific* (exactly how much), *Measurable* (in pounds or kilograms, using weighing scales), *Achievable* (by you), *Relevant* (to you personally) and *Time-Framed* (when, in incremental steps).

Why be so *specific* about your weight-loss goal? Well, because pretty much everything you are, have and do in your life is precise or *specific* – such as your gender, age, height, job, relationships, where you live, etc. So to help your mind get an accurate picture of what you're striving to achieve (rather than a vague, fuzzy picture), you should state your initial weight-loss goal as precisely and specifically as you can, in terms of what weight you want to be and how you want to look and feel like.

As for your weight-loss goal being *measureable*, it is simplicity itself to keep track of your weight: all you need to do is stand on a weighing machine. But you need to keep checking your weight to see how your various efforts are working, on at least a week-by-week basis, making sure you keep an accurate record of your progress.

Remember too that you can always modify your goal as you go along if you discover that you've bitten off too much to achieve, so to speak.

To help get clear and inspired about your goal, you could start by writing in your journal something like:

> *"By ... <insert specific target date here> ... I will have reached my ideal weight of ... <insert specific target weight here>, and I will feel happy with my level of health and fitness, and with how I look, too."*

Bite-Size Tip 33
Consider Weighing Yourself Daily

You weigh yourself to get feedback about your slimming progress. So you should weigh yourself as often as such feedback seems most useful and motivating to you. There is strong scientific evidence to support the effectiveness of daily morning weigh-ins, with daily weighers losing much more weight than weekly weighers.

But if you're not sure about how often you would feel comfortable weighing yourself, ask yourself the following question: However often I chose to weigh myself, and on a particular weighing-in, how motivated will I feel to persevere with my weight-loss plans if I find that I have, a) lost some weight, b) lost no weight, or c) gained some weight? If you can think and feel about the result in each case, in a genuinely constructive and positively motivating way – regardless of whether your daily weight has gone down, up or stayed the same – then you should seriously consider daily weigh-ins, provided, that is, you don't become obsessive about it.

This is how you could think and feel constructively and positively about things with a daily morning weigh-in: if on a given morning you find that you've lost a bit of weight, all well and good; you'll feel good about things. If, on the other hand, you find that you haven't lost any weight since the last weigh-in, then you can still feel okay because you haven't put any extra weight on, and you could let it motivate you to work a little bit harder from that day onwards on your healthier eating and exercise habits. Finally, if you find that you've put a bit of weight back on again, you probably won't feel great about it, but you can nonetheless use your emotional sense of disappointment to motivate yourself to work that bit harder on your healthier eating and exercise habits over the next few days. This positive psychological approach worked really well for me, so I heartily recommend it.

If you do decide to opt for a once weekly weigh-in instead, and if you live a conventional Monday-to-Friday working lifestyle, then studies show that it's likely to be most accurate mid-week a few days after your gluttonous weekends, so do it on Wednesday mornings. This is because it can take two or three days for some waste products to pass through your body from your weekend's excesses, and for your digestive system and metabolism to get back to normal.

But do at least try daily weigh-ins first, maybe for a week or two. Just keep in mind that your daily weight can fluctuate by up to a few pounds from one day to the next, perhaps due to what you've eaten in the previous day or two, as well as due to water retention because of, for instance, higher levels of salt or carbohydrates in your body. If you're a woman, your body will also be slightly heavier during your menstrual periods.

At the end of the day you're looking for a general trend downwards in your weight, week-by-week and month-by-month, so the inevitable daily weight fluctuations either way should be of no concern to you as long as the trend is downwards over time.

To me, the real point of the daily weigh-ins is that it can really help to keep you mentally and emotionally focused and motivated on your weight-loss endeavors, as long as you can think positively about the results each day, regardless of whether your weight has gone down, up or stayed the same. It can all be seen as positive feedback.

FAT FACT

How to Weigh Yourself Properly

For the most accurate results over time:

- Use the same weighing scale every time – using two or three different machines might give you two or three different weights. Not all scales are as accurate as each other.
- To check the accuracy of your weighing machine, weigh a known weight first, such as a bag or two of sugar or a dumbbell or a weight from a weight-lifting set.
- Don't use a cheap and nasty bathroom scale machine – invest in an accurate and well-reviewed gadget, maybe a model which has been endorsed by an organisation such as a health clinic or a respected slimming club.
- Keep the weighing scale on a hard, level and smooth flat surface – not on a soft carpet or any other soft, spongy surface – the rigid outer casing of a weighing scale machine can still deform very slightly if placed on a softer surface when you stand your hefty weight on it, causing it to give an inaccurate reading. If you only have soft flooring where you live, then buy a large, thick and smooth-surfaced ceramic floor tile or a thick, rigid square of wood, large enough to stand the scale on.
- Avoid moving the scale, as this can muck about with the calibration so that it gives varying readings each time you move it and use it. If you have to move the scale, make sure you re-calibrate it again to zero before using it.
- However often you chose to weigh yourself, do it first thing in your day when you get out of bed, *without* wearing any clothes, *after* you've had a pee or a poo or both, and *before* any breakfast food or drink. In other words, weigh yourself at the same time each day, first thing, as soon as you get out of bed, buck naked and empty of bodily waste.

- When you step onto the scale, you want to spread your weight as evenly as possible across the flat surface of the machine. So stand with your feet flat on the machine (not on tip-toes or the balls of your feet or something similarly odd), with your feet a little apart – perhaps the width of one of your feet between them. Some machines have the outline of two feet marked on the surface – obviously place your feet in them if so.

- Keep as perfectly still as you can on the scale until it shows a fixed measurement reading (so don't jiggle about while the machine's thinking).

- If you feel the compulsion to step on and off the scale two or three times within a minute or two to see if your weight reading changes – a sort of cowardly "best out of three" approach – then opt for the heaviest reading; that'll learn you.

- I recommend daily weigh-ins, but if you choose to weigh yourself only once each week, and if you live a conventional Monday-to-Friday working lifestyle, it's probably going to be most accurate first thing Wednesday morning, a few days after your gluttonous weekends.

- If you're one of those crazy health-fanatic lunatics who do rigorous, sweaty exercise first thing in the morning as soon as you leap enthusiastically out of bed to greet the day with rapture, then weigh yourself before and after your exercise – you'll be amazed at how much weight you can lose in just sweat in a long work-out session.

- If your gut is so fat that you can't see around it to the scale's readout display at your feet, ask a trusted fellow human to read it for you ... or use a mirror. You can also buy weighing scales which speak your weight out loud.

- If you really can't understand a word of my instructions here, then you're sure to find a video on how to weigh yourself on the internet.

Bite-Size Tip 34

Aim to Lose One Pound or Less Each Week

Assuming you can be patient enough, aim to lose between about a half pound but no more than about one pound of fatty weight each week on average (that's about a quarter to half a kilogram). This is probably the healthiest strategy to losing weight long-term. Losing such a relatively small amount each week really shouldn't be that hard, once you put your mind to it, because you don't need to reduce your calorific intake and increase your fat-burning exercise by very much. Also, losing no more than one pound of fat each week won't be a real shock to your system, and so shouldn't send your body and brain into a "famine mode". This is when your brain feels that you have been starved, so when food becomes plentiful again, you automatically feel the need to eat extra to build up your fat reserves and prepare for the next famine.

Famine mode is one reason why people who lose weight too quickly often end up even fatter sooner or later.

Another advantage to losing weight slowly is that when you do eventually reach your target weight, you will by then be pretty used to the changes in eating and exercise habits you adopted to lose such a comparatively small amount of weight each week, and so you will only have to modify things just a little bit to maintain your lowest maintainable weight once you reach it.

Bite-Size Tip 35

Measure Your Progress By Your Weight, Clothes Fit and Your Mirror

It's easy to keep an eye on how well your slimming efforts are going by using a combination of weighing yourself regularly on accurate scales, noticing how tightly your clothes fit – and how this fitting changes over time – and seeing how your naked body looks in the mirror. But be really careful with the "mirror test" if you have any reason to believe that you may suffer from a form of Body Dysmorphic Disorder, or BDD; best to seek professional counselling and advice about slimming down if so. BDD is an anxiety disorder related to body image. BDD sufferers don't always see their bodies as they really are, with many thinking they look fat when they are in fact slim (and vice-versa).

FAT FACT
Watch Out for Body Dysmorphic Disorder

Body dysmorphic disorder is an anxiety disorder related to body image. People who have BDD don't always see their bodies as they really are, with many thinking they look fat when they are in fact thin. It can go the other way, too, for some rare BDD sufferers, where they think they look thin when they are in fact fat.

Actually, studies show that fat people who choose to surround themselves socially with other fat people often also think they look thinner than they actually are, though they aren't actually suffering from BDD as such. More likely they just think they look "normal" because everyone else around them looks the same as they do, and they want to be a part of that social group that happens to be made up of fat people.

People with BDD experience unhealthy and unhelpful concerns about their physical appearance which usually have a disruptive effect on their life. Their obsessions about their bodies cause them significant anxiety and they may also develop compulsive behaviours, or routines, to deal with this. In this way, BDD is closely related to obsessive-compulsive disorder (OCD). They may also develop unhealthy habits – such as excessive use of mirrors – to deal with the worries they have about the way they look, or *think* they look, be it fat or thin. These unhealthy habits usually have a significant impact on their ability to carry on with day-to-day life. They may see themselves as significantly disfigured one way or another and are constantly trying to convince themselves and other people of this. At worse, suffering BDD can cause problems such as feelings of shame, guilt and loneliness (some people isolate themselves to avoid situations that cause anxiety or discomfort); depression or anxiety; misuse of alcohol or other drugs; self-harm and even suicidal thoughts.

The problem is, many people who realise that they suffer from some form of BDD don't seek therapeutic help as they feel embarrassed or ashamed, or they're worried that people will judge them, or think they're too vain or some such. This means that many people are likely to experience BDD for a long time before seeking help. But the fact is, BDD can, at the very least, make you unhappy about your body and, at worse, be a serious life-threatening illness, which can even lead to suicide.

Common Symptoms of Body Dysmorphic Disorder

Although everyone who suffers it has their own experience of BDD, there are some common signs. For instance, they will often spend several hours a day thinking negatively about their appearance. They may be concerned about one specific area of their body or they may be worried about several different areas. Common areas of anxiety include: feeling too fat or too skinny, such as around their stomach, thighs and arms; facial features, such as the nose, eyes, hair, chin, skin or lips; particular areas of the body, such as the breasts or genitals; feeling that their body is unbalanced or lacking symmetry; and feeling that one of their features is out of proportion to the rest of the body.

Common compulsive behaviours include: obsessively checking their appearance in mirrors or avoiding mirrors completely; changing their posture or wearing heavy clothes to disguise their shape; constantly comparing themselves with models in magazines, TV and film stars and other slim-looking celebrities, or even people in the street; using heavy make-up when out in public; brushing or styling hair obsessively; seeking constant reassurance about their appearance; checking themselves regularly by feeling their skin with their fingers, particularly around areas they dislike the appearance of; picking their skin to make it smooth; seeking cosmetic surgery or having other types of medical treatment to change the body area of concern.

Recognise any of the signs or behaviours in yourself, by any chance? Interestingly, as I went through the above list of BDD symptoms, signs and behaviours, I couldn't help thinking that quite a few did actually apply to me, albeit, I hope, in a mild and not too unhealthy way. At least I hope so. I suspect it's a bit like people who search the web for symptoms and signs of illnesses, recognise having some or all of them, and so come to think they're suffering from all sorts of conditions. When it comes to it, I imagine lots of unhappy fat people will exhibit one or more of the signs and behaviours for BDD, but not in a particularly unhealthy compulsive or obsessive way, and there's the clue. In other words, it's natural enough to suffer one or more *mild* forms of the symptoms and behaviours of BDD I've listed if you really are unhappy about being fat. But it's not healthy if you experience them in a *compulsive* or *obsessive* way. It's really a matter of degree.

That said, if you do think you may be suffering from BDD, this will significantly influence your motivation for wanting to be slim, almost certainly for unhealthy reasons. And remember, too, that people who do suffer from BDD may not actually be fat or overweight at all – in many cases they aren't – but they just see themselves as fat. So if you think BDD may be involved for you – perhaps because you exhibit many of the compulsive and obsessive signs and behaviours I described – then I very strongly recommend, nay insist, that you seek professional psychotherapeutic help *before* you undertake any slimming down. Because of my own professional biases, I highly recommend seeking a cognitive behavioural therapist who will use scientifically-based, tried-and-tested ways of helping you to discover healthy ways of thinking and feeling about the way you look.

Bite-Size Tip 36
Wear a Non-Elastic Belt

This is another great way of monitoring your weight-loss progress. As you slim down that bulging belly and waistline, you'll find that you can fasten the belt tighter and tighter without suffering or pushing your stomach and lungs up and out of your mouth. And with any luck, the only stretch marks you'll end up with will be around the holes in the belt.

Bite-Size Tip 37

If You Have a Lot of Fat to Lose, Start Out by Setting Small Targets

This can be very effective if the total amount of weight you want to lose seems daunting and overwhelming. If so, then simply chose at first to lose a smaller amount of weight that does feel "do-able" to you – a target weight sub-goal, if you like. Once you've reached that sub-goal, just set another target weight sub-goal to lose a little more weight, and so on and so on, until you eventually reach your final desired target weight.

Indeed, if you have more than just a few pounds or two or three kilograms of fatty weight to lose, then studies show that you're more likely to stay motivated in your slimming efforts if you break your total slimming goal down into smaller chunks of losing only a few pounds or one or two kilograms by a certain date, and focus on that sub-goal. The idea is that you should make precise and written "pre-commitments" to these part-way stages.

For example, if you have a target of 20 pounds of fat to lose over a sensible period of, say, forty weeks or ten months – which works out at two pounds each month – then focus your attention just on the easy goal of losing your two pounds each month, month after month, and forget about your overall, long-distance target.

Using this example, you might write a precise pre-commitment at the start of the month something like: "*I commit to losing just two pounds of fatty weight by the end of this month.*"

Remember to still be *SMART* with your smaller sub-goal targets, i.e. make them *Specific* (exactly how much), *Measurable* (in pounds or kilograms, using weighing scales), *Achievable* (by you), *Relevant* (to you personally) and *Time-Framed* (by when).

Bite-Size Tip 38

Make Your Slimming Goal *Believable, Realistic* and *Achievable* to You

You need to convince yourself beyond any doubt that your slimming goal really is believable, realistic and achievable to you. This is especially important if you have failed to lose weight and keep it off in the past. It can help if you set out to write the answer to a couple of questions in your weight-loss journal. If you have failed with your goal in the past, you might ask yourself something like:

> *"Why do I really believe that I can achieve my weight-loss goal this time?"*

And then,

> *"Is my weight-loss goal really realistic and achievable?"*

You might start off your answer by writing something like:

> *"My weight-loss goal is really realistic and achievable to me because ..."*

Bite-Size Tip 39

You Need Enough Self-Worth to be Happy With Your Weight-Loss

You will only be happy with your weight-loss if you have a healthy level of self-worth – where you really do believe that you deserve to be slim if you want to be. Otherwise, you risk going through all that toil and trouble to lose weight only to find that you are no more satisfied, content or happy with your slimmer body after all.

To help determine and nurture a healthy level of self-worth, answer the following two interrelated questions:

> "Why should I feel that I'm a good enough, worthy and valuable human being who deserves to lose weight and be happy?"

> "Why shouldn't I be good enough and deserve to achieve my weight-loss goal and be happy?"

Affirm to yourself these words, believing them as strongly as you can:

> "I genuinely feel that I'm a good enough, worthy and valuable human being who deserves to lose weight and be happy."

Bite-Size Tip 40

If You Have Doubts, then "Fake It Till You Make It" Or "Act As If" You Can Lose Weight

If you harbour any doubts whatsoever about your ability to lose weight and slim down then you seriously risk sabotaging your success. Perhaps you are not fully convinced that your weight-loss goal really is believable, realistic and achievable, or perhaps you consciously or unconsciously don't think that you "deserve" or are "worthy" or "good enough" to be slim.

If you believe this could be the case with you, then, as convincingly as you possibly can, just "act as if" you have no doubts whatsoever about any of this stuff, and "fake it till you make it". After all, armed with all the scientifically-proven tools and techniques you now have at your fingertips, you have every reason not to have any doubts.

For example, you could tell yourself, every day, out loud and to your face in the mirror, using bold, assertive speech and pointing at yourself with a prodding index-finger, speaking with heart-felt conviction, that you can reach your goal. You could say something like:

> "Of course my slimming goal is believable, realistic and achievable to me! Why shouldn't it be, especially now I know so many evidence-based ways of using my brain and behaviours?"

… and maybe too:

> "Of course I'm worthy, good enough and deserve to lose weight and be slim! Why not, especially now I know where I went wrong in past failed attempts?"

Consider saying these things to your partner/spouse/a trusted friend or two as well, for added impact.

123

Bite-Size Tip 41

Make Sure Your Weight-Loss Goal is Really Relevant to You Personally

It's really important that your weight-loss goal is all about *you*, and not about what anyone else thinks. The fact is, you're more likely to fail if you're slimming down because someone else thinks you should, which might mean that you yourself are not personally convinced that you need to lose weight.

NOTE: This is closely related to what I say under Bite-Size Tip 23: Make Sure You Want to Lose Weight for the Right Personal Reasons and Bite-Size-Tip 26: Identify Your True Reasons for Wanting yo Lose Weight, both in Topic 1: Losing Weight Has to Matter a Lot to You Personally.

To help establish if your weight-loss goal really is about you, in your weight-loss journal make sure you answer these questions (if you haven't already):

"Who am I really losing weight for?"

"What is important to me personally about achieving my weight-loss goal?"

"What will achieving my weight-loss goal do for me personally – in what ways will I benefit?"

"What are the real reasons I want to lose weight?"

As I just implied, the chances are you've answered these questions already under other activities, but it's still worth going through them here.

Bite-Size Tip 42

Define *When* You Want to Reach Your Target Weight

Work out how much weight you need to lose to reach your target weight. Then, aiming to lose my recommended healthy average of *less* than one pound each week (less than half a kilo) – preferably about half-a-pound – you should be able to calculate precisely how many weeks it will take you to reach your target weight and hence your target date.

I say "precisely", but don't get too obsessed about losing the weight precisely by this date. I've argued elsewhere the healthy reasons for losing weight *slowly* over time – certainly no more than a pound each week – but things may well work out differently for you. Obviously, you may reach your target weight sooner than expected, especially if you lose, say, four pounds of fat each month. This is fine, as long as you then give serious attention to how you will maintain your new healthy weight in the *long-term* – most people don't, and just revert back towards their old unhealthier eating and exercise habits.

However, more often people don't lose the weight as quickly as they had hoped, especially if they have two or more stone (about 13 kilos or more) to lose. This is usually due to a variety of factors, so it's important to be flexible with your mindset here. If you find that you're losing weight more slowly than you hoped, then try to work out why, learn the lessons, maybe adjust your weight-loss approach and then re-set your target date for when you hope to reach your desired weight, perhaps based on your overall average rate of weight loss until now.

Most importantly, be kind, understanding and compassionate towards yourself for not losing as much weight as you had hoped by now; you're only human, after all.

Bite-Size Tip 43

Focus on How Far You've Got to Go to Reach Your Weight-Loss Goal, Not on How Far You've Come

Scientific research suggests that it can help you stay more motivated if you focus on how many pounds you still have to lose to reach your goal, rather than on how many pounds you have lost already. The danger with focusing on how much weight you've lost to date is that while it might make you feel good about your achievement, it might also make you feel too complacent and smug, which may cause you to lose sight of how far you still have to go.

All this can serve to weaken your motivation to keep shedding the pounds you still need to lose to reach your goal weight. So keep your focus mainly on the rest of the journey, and not so much on how far you've come so far.

This advice may, on the face of it at least, seem to contradict the advice I give in 'Tip 14: Celebrate Your Weight-Loss Successes'. But if you think about it, there's no reason that both shouldn't work well, especially if you think of each of your successes as being milestones which remind you not only of how far you've come but also, more importantly, on how much further you still have to go. This all reminds me of a long walk I sometimes do along the edge of a loch in Scotland near to where I live, which has milestone signs every mile or two along the path telling you how far you've come and how far you still have to go. I get a sense of pleasure and reward every time I reach a sign, with that sense of pleasure and reward increasing for each successive milestone sign as I get ever nearer to my final destination.

Bite-Size Tip 44

Your Weight-Loss Goal Statement Should Stimulate Multi-Sensory Thinking and Emotions

Written and spoken words of affirmation – called *positive self-statements* – are probably not going to be enough to help you reach your weight-loss goal. That said, affirmations can work well for many people when combined with the sort of positive-action tools and tips you are learning about in this book. To drive your weight-loss goal as deeply as possible into your unconscious mind – and so to elicit the powerful aid of the unconscious – you need to harness all your senses. You need to think about, write down, and recite your weight-loss goal statement in such a way that it clearly and vividly stimulates as many of your main senses and positive emotions as possible whenever you think about it. So, whenever you read and think about your slimming goal statement, ideally it needs to implicitly or explicitly stimulate in your mind something visual (seeing), olfactory (smell), gustatory (taste), auditory (sound), kinaesthetic (touch/bodily sensation), as well as positive emotional sensations that the statement represents and brings to mind for you, on a deep, personal level.

Visualising, "sensorising" and "emotionalising" getting slimmer

In your weight-loss journal, re-write your weight-loss goal statement into the present tense, as if you've just reached your target weight. Imagine this success as vividly and as strongly as you possibly can. Really immerse yourself in and relish the imaginary experience of being slimmer and fitter. Then, while enjoying this blissful state, creatively and richly imagine, and write down in your journal, all of your multi-sensory and emotional impressions that are a direct or indirect result of you slimming down, using something like the following ideas:

"I see … <insert what you would be seeing on reaching your slimming goal>".

"I hear … <insert what you would be hearing on reaching your slimming goal, such as what people might say>".

"I touch/feel … <insert what you would be touching/feeling/handling on reaching your slimming goal>".

"I smell … <insert what you would be smelling on reaching your slimming goal>".

"I taste … <insert what you would be tasting/eating on reaching your slimming goal>".

"My body feels … <insert how your body feels and your body posture on reaching your slimming goal>".

"My emotions are … <insert what and how you would be feeling emotionally on reaching your slimming goal>".

"I am … <insert the things you would be doing on reaching your slimming goal>".

"I am saying … <insert what you would be saying to yourself and others on reaching your slimming goal>".

"Other people are … <insert what other people are doing and saying as a result of you achieving your slimming goal, including your partner/spouse, friends and relatives>".

"I can hear the music … <insert your triumphant slimming soundtrack on reaching your slimming goal>".

Topic 3: What are the Obstacles that Stop You Getting Slim?

Bite-Size Tip 45
Identify the *Navigable* Obstacles and Barriers

It's important to be realistically optimistic about being able to achieve your slimming goal. But part of this involves being realistic, too, about situations that will challenge you along your journey and how you might deal with them when they arise. You are bound to come up against obstacles and various other barriers to slimming down, including temptations and "triggers" that make you eat too much. If you can clearly identify such potential barriers, the better prepared you will be to overcome, avoid or remove them entirely when they do, almost inevitably, crop up.

To help identify issues before they happen, jot down and answer the following interrelated and overlapping questions in your weight-loss journal:

"How, why, when, and in what ways did I get fat in the first place?"

"What has stopped me achieving my slimming goal to date?"

"What might stand between me and my slimming goal now?"

"What other things might hold me back from getting slim?"

"What sort of things could go wrong?"

"Do I have any thoughts that are sabotaging my plans, or am I engaging in any form of faulty thinking that stops me losing weight?" (See Tip 50 about this.)

"What triggers make me eat too much that I need to be be prepared and watch out for?"

Bite-Size Tip 46

Monitor those Eating "Triggers"

Another way to spot potential obstacles to your slimming success is to carefully watch out for and record all the "triggers" that make you want to eat too much. These might be certain situations, times or places in your day-to-day work and home life. Then set about ways of reducing or even cutting out your exposure to such unhelpful triggering events. If neither of those is an option, set about changing the way you respond to the triggers. See Tip 48 for ideas.

Bite-Size Tip 47
Use "Back from the Future" Thinking

Yet another novel way of helping you to spot potential obstacles to your weight-loss plans is to use something called "Back from the Future" thinking.

The idea here is that you first imagine, as vividly and as richly as you can – using as many senses as possible in your imagination – that you have already achieved your weight-loss goal, and that you now look and feel as slim and as healthy as desired. Imagine as strongly as you can how successfully slimming down like this will make you feel emotionally. While in this blissful vision of the future, "look back" along the rocky road to your successful weight loss, and list all the obstacles, temptations and setbacks you had to deal with and overcome, and how you managed it. And don't forget to write it all down in your weight-loss journal for future reference.

Bite-Size Tip 48

Plan in Advance to Replace an Unhelpful Triggered Behaviour With a Helpful One

To plan in advance how to replace one triggered behavioural habit with another, it is helpful to learn about something technically known as "if-then" implementation intention planning. Many studies have proven this to be a very powerful tool for habit-change.

The basic idea of "if-then" implementation intention planning is, as the name suggests, to plan, in advance, *how* you will avoid an unhelpful or counterproductive behavioural habit (the "…-then" bit) that is usually triggered by a particular situation or event (the "if-…" bit).

There are three types of "if-then" implementation intention planning strategies you can use: in order of proven ease of implementation and thus effectiveness, they are: *replacement*, *ignore* and *negation* planning.

The type that seems to work best for most people and situations seems to be replacement "if-then" planning, where you *replace* the unhelpful habit with a more helpful or constructive behaviour. When it comes to changing your eating habits, you need to decide what helpful alternative habit you will adopt instead of an unhelpful triggered eating habit. It is best if the new helpful or constructive habit will in some way meet the same physical, emotional or mental needs as the unhelpful habit currently does. For example, you might plan: "*If* I feel a bit peckish between meals, *then* I'll just drink a large glass of water and maybe I'll make like a rabbit and munch a carrot or two if need be" (instead of the usual unhelpful fatty or sugary snack you ate until now when you were making like a fat pig).

Next best is *ignore* "if-then" planning, where you somehow block-out or otherwise ignore the temptation of the counterproductive behaviour altogether; this requires more willpower. For instance, you might plan in your weight-loss journal: "*If* I feel a bit peckish between meals, *then* I'll just ignore the feeling." Good luck with that. Alternatively, you might be better here to sneak in a *replacement* distraction technique instead, planning something like: "*If* I feel a bit peckish between meals, *then* I'll do something to take my mind off it, such as watch a bit of TV, call someone for a chat or go for a walk."

Finally, and least effective, is *negation* "if-then" planning, where you focus your thinking on the unhelpful or counterproductive behaviour you *won't* or *don't* want to do. For example, you might plan: "*If* I feel a bit peckish between meals, *then* I won't eat the usual fatty or sugary snack I ate until now." For many people, this *negation* if-then planning can even be counterproductive sometimes, not least because you have to keep in mind what you *don't* want to do – so it's probably best to avoid this if possible.

Arguably, for most people, it's best to focus on what you *will* do, and not on what you won't do. So, for a given trigger situation, try to come up with a *replacement* "if-then" implementation intention plan first. If that fails, then settle on an *ignore* "if-then" plan instead, and only resort to a *negation* "if-then" plan as a last resort. As in the examples above, you could word each of your "if-then" plans along the lines of:

> "*IF* I feel the urge to...<insert counterproductive behaviour here>, *THEN* I will...<insert constructive behaviour here> instead."

It's best to recite out-loud to yourself (and others) your chosen "if-then" plan a few times. To maximise the effectiveness of this, speak with strong and convincing intonation and emphasis, and use plenty of visualisation or "sensorisation" (preferably using all your senses), plus put in some heart-felt emotion and intention. Good luck.

Bite-Size Tip 49
Think "DoubleThink"

"DoubleThink" is where you hold two seemingly opposing beliefs or ideas about your slimming efforts and yet accept *both* as true.

Here's what you do: if you haven't done so already, list all the benefits that will result from you slimming down, in order of importance to you. Making the list is a very important exercise in itself, not least because it can help motivate you. Remember also to write it all down in your weight-loss journal; that's very important, too. Then, if you haven't done so already, make a list of all the obstacles and hurdles you are likely to meet as you try to slim down, again in order of significance.

Now, to use "DoubleThink", you reflect deeply on your first listed benefit, making sure to work out precisely *how* it will make your life better and more enjoyable, etc. Then *immediately* after this, think deeply about the biggest obstacle to your slimming success, focusing in particular on what you will do if you meet that hurdle (such as an "if-then" implementation intention plan; see the previous tip). Repeat the same process for the second most significant benefit and second greatest potential hurdle, then the third most significant benefit and third hurdle, and so on.

"Doublethink" possibly works because of the way it balances benefits with assessment of problems. So in terms of weight-loss, the benefits of reaching your slimming goal is balanced against the realistic expectation of problems that could be met along the way, and how you can overcome them.

Bite-Size Tip 50
Beware of Unhelpful Automatic Thoughts

You need to watch out for any automatic beliefs or thoughts you may have that one way or another sabotage, hijack or hinder your weight-loss efforts. Such thoughts happen most often when you're feeling highly emotionally, particularly if you feel stressed or upset, but they can also sometimes pop up when you are feeling good, too. At the time, you fully believe these sabotaging ideas, but under closer scrutiny they don't hold up to objective reality, and so they prove unhelpful to your slimming efforts.

Such automatic sabotaging beliefs and thoughts contain one or more thinking errors, such as:

- *all-or-nothing* – you think in simple "black and white" or "one extreme to the other" terms
- *catastrophising* – you imagine that the worst will happen
- *fortune telling* about the future – you expect certain things will happen, but your predictions are not based on solid evidence
- *mind reading* what other people think – again, what you imagine is not based on solid evidence
- *unfair comparisons* – you compare particular things or situations in ways that are not merited
- "*shoulding*" and "*musterbating*" – your thinking is based around authoritative-sounding, assertive statements containing such words as "should", "must", "ought" and "can't", which are not in keeping with your own beliefs or values (the obvious challenge here is "should", "must", "ought" or "can't" according to what authority?).
- *emotional reasoning* – your justify yourself with emotions rather than reason
- *arbitrary rules* – you make up rules for yourself that may not be true or valid

Once you recognise or even just suspect that your mind is coming up with such sabotaging beliefs and thinking errors, you can challenge and overcome them by asking yourself one or more of the following sorts of questions:

- Is this belief or thought helping me to lose weight? If not, why not?
- What is the most realistic and likely outcome of acting on this belief or thought?
- Is my belief or thought logical?
- Is it realistic?
- Is it always definitely true?
- What evidence is there that it might not be true, or not completely true?
- Would a scientist agree with my logic and reasoning behind my belief?
- Where is the evidence for my belief or thought?
- Where is my belief or thought written down, apart from inside my head?
- Am I likely to feel guilt, shame, regret or any other bad emotions later on if I act on this belief or thought?
- Would my friends agree with my idea?
- What would I say to a friend who held such a belief or thought?
- Does everyone share my attitude? If not, why not?
- Is there another healthier explanation or another healthier way of thinking about this belief?
- What is the effect on my dieting of my believing this thought and what could be the effect on my dieting if I change my thinking?

Bite-Size Tip 51
Strengthen Your Willpower Muscles

Dealing with the all-too many obstacles to your weight-loss efforts, such as sabotaging thoughts, eating triggers and other culinary temptations, sometimes needs huge amounts of self-control or willpower. Self-control or willpower seems to be a limited resource for many people. It can be used up and can run low, if not run completely dry, making it even harder, or downright impossible, to resist the urge for unhealthy habits or overeating.

However, scientists have shown that if you can convince yourself strongly enough and believe that your willpower is not going to run out, and that you have all the willpower you need and then some, you can actually persevere much longer with various willpower-needing tasks than people who don't share that mindset. Scientists have also shown that it can be useful to think of our willpower as like a muscle, which behaves just like any other muscle in our body. So, just like real muscles, if you don't give your willpower muscle much use or "exercise" it can become weak and flabby, so to speak. But if you use it regularly, giving it lots and lots of "exercise", it will grow stronger and stronger. So the more you use your willpower to resist those foody temptations, the easier it gets over time.

If you give in to a temptation your willpower will not become stronger and so you will not be better able to resist the next time you're exposed to the same temptation. Even worse, it turns out that giving in to the temptation may well just weaken your willpower and so make it more likely that you will give in to the same temptation again in the future. So if you want to lose weight and keep it off, you need to take every chance you can to strengthen your willpower muscle, and believe it is strong. In this way you can wither and weaken your "giving in" muscle.

Here's a selection of cognitive and behavioural techniques you can use to boost your suffering self-control and willpower at once:

- You may be able to boost your willpower just by *believing* – with all your heart and soul – that willpower is not a finite or limited resource, and that you really do have all the willpower you need, and more in reserve, too. The fact that this positive thinking is supported by a number of scientific studies from around the globe should make it much easier to believe it, that you have all the willpower you need, and even more. So go ahead, and really adopt the belief that you have all the willpower you need, more so, in fact, because you almost certainly do. It may take a bit of time, repetition and practice for your belief to work, but this is well worth persevering with, if you can muster the willpower to do so, of course.

- If just believing that you have enough willpower isn't working for you right now, probably the next easiest thing to do is give your seemingly tired and flagging old willpower a good, long, well-deserved rest, just like you would with tired and worn-out muscles. In other words, don't do anything that requires any willpower to do.

- To give your self-control and willpower an immediate boost, think really hard about someone you know who has oodles, nay, even an over-abundance of self-control and willpower. Think of several people if you can. And if you don't know anyone personally, think of someone you've heard about, even a fictional character or a few if need be. Either way, as richly and as vividly as you can, imagine them using their iron-strong willpower to get things done.

- Doing something that puts you in a cheerful mood can also raise your willpower levels. Indulge in anything that really lifts your spirits and makes you feel great. Pretty much anything that enhances your positive emotions can help restore your willpower strength, though avoid alcohol as it actually weakens your self-control and willpower, instead of strengthening it.

In the longer-term, you can build up your willpower muscle by giving it regular workouts. In other words, just like we strengthen muscles in our body by using them, we can strengthen our willpower muscle by doing things that require some degree of willpower, however small. This can include regularly taking on even very small challenges that need us to do something that we'd honestly rather not really do, and hence need some willpower to get through. And interestingly, and rather encouragingly, it doesn't have to be something to do with your weight-loss endeavours either.

Scientists suggest that to strengthen your self-control and willpower, you can choose just about anything you can do regularly as long as it involves using some amount of willpower itself to overcome the urge not to do it – in other words, do something you wouldn't usually do, or something you'd probably rather not do, or something you find a bit of a challenge to do.

It can be really hard to lose weight, but with enough willpower, it is definitely possible. However, it is not the best strategy to rely on willpower *alone*, because your willpower may simply not be strong enough when faced with some obstacles, barriers, or temptations. Even if your willpower is strong enough, it can take a lot of energy and effort to maintain it, especially in the long-term. That's where the strength of your *motivation* or reasons to lose weight can make the real difference between success and failure. We'll consider how to get more motivated next.

Bite-Size Tip 52
Get More Motivated

Along with willpower and forming new, healthy habits (see Tip 53), motivation is one of the keys to taking action; any action, that is, so not just for weight loss. Your motivation to act is fuelled by your important or compelling reason or reasons – conscious or unconscious – for choosing whether or not to take an action. Each of your motivating reasons is linked to an emotional feeling, longing, desire, drive, urge or willingness to achieve something. In fact, the more personal emotion involved, the stronger and more powerful your motivation will be.

If we think of motivation as a force behind our choices, then the strength of our reasons for the choice can be thought of as the strength of the motivating force. In other words, the stronger your reasons are for your choice to lose weight, the stronger will be your motivation. And the stronger your motivation, the more likely you are to make the necessary choices and take action. This is why taking the trouble to explore and identify your *true, personal* and *emotionally-loaded* reasons for wanting to lose weight is so important. Identifying your genuine motivating reason for wanting to lose weight is one of the most important things you can do to maximise your chances of success, especially in the long term.

Your motivation to act, behave or do a particular thing comes from two main sources: internal to you (also called *intrinsic* motivation) and external to you (also called *extrinsic* motivation). They are both important for reaching your weight-loss goal, just for different reasons.

Internal motivation is when you're motivated to act by internal, subjective factors personal to you – both conscious and unconscious – such as your own personal beliefs, your core values, the "life stories" you tell yourself and live by, your patterns of thinking and behaving, your models of reality, ideas, immediate needs, emotions, aims, "life rules", goals, and your inner expectations that you impose upon yourself. You're internally motivated to take action because the goal or outcome is important to you personally, for whatever reason. When you're internally motivated it means you're *not* doing whatever it is so as to get something from the outside world as such, like approval or acceptance from others or some other external reward or benefit; rather it's about meeting your own internal beliefs, values, needs and wants. Moreover, you're internally motivated to perform an action or behaviour when you enjoy the action or behaviour *in and of itself,* so the inspiration for you to act is found in the action or behaviour itself, sometimes even with no other aim in mind. Internal motivation drives you to do things just for the pure pleasure of it, or because you believe it is a "good" or "right" thing to do for you, which you enjoy doing just for its own sake, where even the process itself is often enjoyable to do, even regardless of the final outcome. This is a case where the journey really is as rewarding as the destination, if not more so.

Internal motivation is so powerful because it's being driven by your usually unconscious requirement to fulfill your basic or fundamental human needs, especially your fundamental human psychological or emotional needs, such as the need for a sense of competence and autonomy in things you do, or the need for a meaning and purpose in life.

External motivation is when you're motivated to act by objective or external factors, outside of yourself, so to speak. So you're motivated to act by external rewards, rules, regulations, deadlines, obligations, family, friendships and wider social and cultural norms, gender roles, perceived societal or workplace status, money, fame, grades, approval, praise, and all other outer expectations that others impose upon you one way or another. External motivation drives you to do things for external tangible reasons, rewards, benefits or pressures, rather than just for the sheer pleasure of doing whatever it is for its own sake, or for some other internal motivation. A potential problem with being motivated solely by external motivating factors is that if the external factors change, weaken or disappear entirely, so too might your motivation change, weaken or disappear. This is one reason why it can be better to be more internally motivated.

In fact, for most people it seems that when they're adequately internally motivated, consciously or not, then they have much less need, if any, for any external motivation. An obvious example is when you want to do something you enjoy on your own (I'll leave you to think of examples here). This is another reason why it is generally better to be more internally motivated than externally motivated.

So get as clear as you can about precisely why you want to lose weight and get slim in the first place. What are your real or true motivating reasons? Do you really, truly, absolutely, definitely, cross-your-heart-and-hope-to-die actually want or even need to lose weight? Are your reasons internal or external motivations? What fundamental human needs do your motivating reasons seem to meet or satisfy, in particular your needs for a sense of competence and autonomy in things you do, and the need for a sense of relatedness or connection to the people around you? What about satisfying other needs: for positive emotions much of the time; for a sense of security; for intimacy; for resilience; for vitality; for high self-esteem; for a sense of achievement; to receive and give attention; and for a sense of control? How many of these and other psychological needs do your motivating reasons for wanting to lose weight meet and satisfy? The more, the better. There's more about fundamental human needs and their impact on weight loss in Tip 24.

So it's no exaggeration to say that going through the activity of identifying precisely *why* you want to lose weight, carefully and thoughtfully, is absolutely crucial if you want to lose weight successfully and keep it off long-term. That fact is, if your motivating reasons for wanting to lose weight are not clear enough or are not important or strong enough to you, then you probably won't succeed long-term, if at all. In other words, *not* having clear or important or strong enough motivating reasons for wanting to lose weight could well prove to be an almost insurmountable obstacle and barrier to you successfully reaching and keeping at your target weight. That's precisely why you *must* give this activity proper attention. And write it all down, too, in your weight-loss journal.

In conclusion here, if you've diligently gone through all of my recommended activities, you should by now have a list of deeply thought-through motivating reasons for why you really do want to lose weight. You should have a good sense of the deeply personal and emotionally-loaded, internal and external motivating factors involved. You should also have some insight about which of your own fundamental human needs your motivating reasons are trying to meet. This really is very powerful and useful stuff, and it most definitely will help you to stay on track towards your weight-loss goal. This is especially true if you think about your motivating reasons often, preferably at least once or twice each day, and particularly at times when you're finding it difficult to stick with your weight-loss plans because of obstacles or temptations.

When you find your true and deep, emotionally-loaded and personal motivations to do something, you no longer need to rely solely on your willpower, if at all. You do whatever it is because you really want to, not because you have to, and this is usually so much stronger, easier and longer-lasting than relying on willpower alone. But you have to nonetheless accept that sometimes your motivation will weaken for one reason or another, and that's when your willpower can come to the rescue. So make sure you work on building up your willpower muscles, too.

Furthermore, as with many things, when it comes to adopting new and healthier lifestyle habits to help you lose weight and keep it lost, you need to keep repeating things regularly and consistently as a good way to build and strengthen the habits. Again, that's where your willpower can prove really effective alongside and supporting your motivation, especially at times when your motivation is feeling weak. When you repeat a pattern or thought or behaviour often enough, in the right way, it becomes a habit. And the brilliant and even exciting thing about strong habits is that they need little or even no willpower or motivation to do, because the "habit circuits" in your brain take the strain. We turn to habits in the next section.

Bite-Size Tip 53
Break Bad Habits and Hone Healthy Habits

You can greatly assist your slimming efforts by creating new, helpful eating and exercise habits, and breaking old unhelpful habits. From your brain's point of view, there's no such thing as a "bad" habit; they all serve what your brain thinks is a "useful" purpose in some way, however misguided or misplaced that may be in fact. So it's more useful to think of "bad" habits as being "unhelpful" (or "unhealthy") in terms of achieving your goal, while "good" habits are "helpful" (or "healthy").

A habit is made up of three main parts: a cue, a routine and a reward. All habits lead to a benefit or reward of some kind; otherwise your brain wouldn't engage in them. The reward could simply be that the habit frees up your brain's processing power for other more important things, like staying alive. So, first we experience a cause or cue, which sets off a drive or craving for the benefit or reward, and which the brain recognises as a trigger to go into automatic mode and choose which habit routine to use to gain the desired reward. The habitual routine response triggered by the cue might be physical, mental or emotional, or more likely a combination. Finally there is the benefit or reward, which, if good enough, helps your brain decide to use the same response to the same cue again in the future. An important thing to reiterate here is that the cue must trigger a craving for the reward, thus driving the habit. As we repeat a specific response to a specific cue, the overall cue-response behaviour becomes laid down as a "chunk" of habitual actions in special "habit circuits" in the brain. Once fully laid down, the habitual behaviour becomes automatic and probably impossible to totally erase, though it is possible to break, suppress or neutralise the effects of an existing habit by overwriting it with another new habit which reaps the same reward or better.

When it comes to breaking, suppressing or neutralising unhelpful habits, try the following:

- **Identify the habit** – Identify exactly what the habit is and the components that make up the habit; in other words, what is the cause, trigger or *cue*; what is the habitual *routine* response to the cue; and what is the benefit, pleasure or *reward* you get from the habit? So spend some time carefully analysing your habitual behaviour, asking questions like: What is the habit? When do you do it? Why? What is the cue? What is the usual habitual routine response to the cue? How does it make me feel – what's the reward? When isolating the habit cue, remember that it may be made up of one or more factors, including: time, location, other people, your emotional state and another preceding action or habit that came before the cue.

- **Remove the cue** – If possible, remove the cue, because if there's no cue to trigger the habit, then there's no need to worry about the habit, is there? Many people find that removing the cue is the easiest way of getting rid of an unhelpful habit, if removing the cue is possible, of course. For example, if every time you notice the biscuit container (the cue) when you have a cup of tea it triggers a craving to eat some biscuits with your tea, then don't have a biscuit container full of biscuits (remove the cue), at least not one in plain sight.

- **Think of a new habit routine** – If you can't or don't want to avoid the cue, then think of a new, helpful habitual routine to overwrite, override and otherwise usurp the current unhelpful routine. Remember, if the new, helpful routine is going to take root, it will have to be able to deliver the same reward experience, or better, as the unwanted, unhelpful routine you're trying to overcome.

- **Practice the new habit** – When trying to replace an existing unhelpful habit with a new helpful habit, work hard to engage and practice the new habit as often as possible every time you encounter the triggering cue.

If you want to start and establish a new, helpful habit:

- **Choose a clear and simple triggering cue, and a clear benefit or reward** – Ideally, in time the cue must trigger a strong desire or craving for the reward. Remember that craving drives the three-step habit loop: *cue – routine – reward*; the stronger the craving, the stronger the habit.

- **Consider your motivation** – Why do you want the new habit? Is the reason strong enough? This is important for motivation and willpower.

- **Have a plan to get the habit going** – An ideal time to establish a new habit is immediately after or, failing that, immediately before, an existing habit has occurred. It is even better if you can link the new habit with another existing habit, which has a similar reward or aim in mind.

- **Satisfaction with the new habit is key to keeping it going** – In other words, does the new habit reap the benefit or reward you want? If you don't feel that you're getting a strong enough reward, it's going to be hard to continue the new, healthy habit. Ideally, you want the habit to eventually become intrinsically motivated, which means you do it – and hopefully actually enjoy doing it – for its own sake, rather than for some external or extrinsic reason, such as to please someone else or because you feel that you "should" or "must" adopt the habit.

- **Try changing something if the habit doesn't seem to be sticking and taking root** – A habit may not stick and take root for at least three main reasons:
  1) the triggering cue isn't clear or strong enough;
  2) the motivating reason, benefit or reward isn't strong enough; and
  3) the habitual routine response isn't effective enough to deliver the desired reward.

In conclusion, however well you manage to replace your old, unhealthy eating and exercise habits that helped to get you fat in the first place by adopting new, healthy lifestyle habits, you must be on constant guard against your older, unhealthy habits re-awakening and re-asserting themselves. They will if you give them less than even half a chance, so be very wary.

Bite-Size Tip 54
Prepare for *Red for Danger* Days

Watch out for and prepare yourself as best you can for those days in your diary on which you can expect your weight-loss efforts to be particularly challenged in one way or another. For example, you might be about to head off on a business trip staying in a hotel, or maybe a day-trip with your family, or maybe you're due to spend a weekend with friends, or, dreaded by many dieters most of all, the Christmas festivities are looming on the calendar's horizon.

If you forewarn yourself about such potentially challenging events and forearm yourself with the best ways to meet the challenge, you will be prepared to deal with the temptations as they arise. Try to establish helpful habits beforehand, accept that you might not meet your monthly weight-loss target that month, and don't get depressed or disappointed if that happens. Account in your diary for these sorts of challenging events and don't set your weight-loss target too optimistically low for those periods.

Bite-Size Tip 55
Lose Weight to Gain Weight

Suppose you have an upcoming event where you're pretty sure that you're likely to eat, drink and make merry to excess – such as a holiday, a weekend feasting with friends, or the Christmas festivities – and that you will almost definitely gain back a few pounds of fat. If you really don't want to face this disheartening consequence that will push back your target weight date, then one option worth considering is to lose extra weight during the few weeks leading up to the event.

All you need to do is lose the additional few pounds you think you're likely to gain by the end of the event. For example, if you think you're likely to gain back, say, three pounds in weight, then aim to shed those extra three pounds immediately prior to the event, in *addition* to your normal weight-loss target. The more weeks you spread that additional three pounds over before the event, the easier it will be to lose it along with your usual weight-loss target. As an added bonus, many people find that losing weight "in-advance" like this effectively gives them permission to fully enjoy and indulge themselves without fear of future guilt, shame or regret.

Bite-Size Tip 56

Use Mental Rehearsal to Prepare for Challenging Situations

Suppose you know that you're soon going to be in a situation which will sorely challenge your dieting or exercise willpower and motivation, and so, too, your ability to replace an old unhelpful eating or exercise habit with a shiny, new, healthy one. Well, you can very effectively help boost your willpower and resolve by mentally rehearsing what you will do when the situation arises.

In other words, in your mind's eye you imagine going through the behaviour that will help you during the challenging event – as vividly and using as many senses as possible – before the event occurs. It can work even better if you "emotionalise" the mental rehearsal, imagining as strongly as you can how great you will feel when you adopt the new helpful habit. And it can be even more effective still if you repeat the whole mental rehearsal again and again, with all its rich sensory and emotional detail, as many times as you possibly can before the actual event.

Bite-Size Tip 57
Feed on Your Guilt, Shame and Regret

When we give in to a temptation that we shouldn't have, we often end up feeling rubbish or bad about ourselves for giving in, for example feeling guilt, shame or regret. But we can use these negative feelings to our advantage.

When faced with a tempting pleasure or habit, before you give in and indulge, it can help you to resist if you first stop dead in your tracks, and remind yourself how bad you'll feel about yourself afterwards if you do give in. If it's a temptation you've failed to resist in the past, remind yourself how rubbish and guilty you felt the times you gave in before, but how good you felt the times you did manage to resist, assuming you did manage to resist at all in the past, of course. If not, think about how good you *will* feel resisting this time, not least because this may be the very first time you manage it, but also because you will stop feeling bad by giving in like you did all the other times.

The important idea here is to link how you choose to respond to the temptation *now* with the potentially negative emotional effects *afterwards*, especially your senses of guilt, shame or regret at giving in to the temptation. If you can recognise and accept that giving in and indulging in the pleasure now will make you feel worse afterwards, then the urge to give in weakens or, put another way, the urge to resist grows stronger.

It will be even better if you can accept that successfully exerting your self-control or willpower becomes the real pleasure, and the unhelpful temptation becomes the source of the painful guilt, shame and regret.

Bite-Size Tip 58
Are You *Really* Hungry?

Many overweight people actually find it very hard to tell the difference between feeling genuinely *metabolically* hungry, when their body needs nutrients, and just having the desire to eat due to pleasure-seeking or *hedonic* hunger. Some such dieters report feeling hungry all the time, and some others report *hardly ever* feeling hungry as such; they mostly eat for other reasons such as habit, or a desire or craving to eat something such as chocolate, ice cream or pizza. In both cases, the well-intentioned weight-loss advice of eating whenever you feel hungry, or *only* eating when you feel hungry, is unhelpful or even useless.

One very good way of learning the difference between metabolic hunger and the craving associated with emotionally-driven hedonic hunger is to monitor how you feel in three different situations:

- Go all day without eating and notice how you feel before your evening meal; this "feeling" is most likely metabolic hunger, especially if you feel that eating anything at all would do.

- Wait for the time when you've had a good-sized meal – such as a starter and main course – but still desire to eat even more, such as a dessert. So soon after such a good-sized meal, when you surely can't still be metabolically hungry, this is most likely just a desire to eat due to hedonic hunger, especially if you desire something specific to eat, such as only one particular thing on the dessert menu, and nothing else appeals to you.

- Keep a look out for when you feel a really strong urge or driving need to eat, especially when that urge is accompanied by a feeling of tension or anxiety of some sort, and perhaps, too, an almost unpleasant longing or yearning sensation in your mouth, throat, stomach, head or elsewhere in your body; this is most likely a *craving to eat*, probably due to hedonic hunger, especially if you crave something specific to eat, such as something sugary or fatty like chocolate, biscuits, cake or ice cream.

In all three situations note how your stomach feels, how "hungry" you feel, and any other associated sensations in your mind, mouth, throat and in other parts of your body. Note such things just before you eat, then about half-way during your eating, then immediately or very soon after you've finished, and finally one or two hours after eating as well.

If, after all that, you still can't learn to tell the difference between metabolic and hedonic hunger, then you're best advised to stick to a pre-determined diet and eating plan of set meals at set times of the day. This applies especially when you're in the process of losing weight, but make sure to include the odd deviation from your plan now and again, particularly once you've reached your desired target weight range. Everything in moderation, remember.

Bite-Size Tip 59
Learn to Tolerate Hunger, Desire and Craving

To be able to successfully tolerate and resist hunger, desires and cravings you will need to experiment with a range of cognitive and behavioural tools and techniques – in other words, tricks of thinking, feeling and acting – to discover what works best for you in particular situations. Remember that although you're feeling hungry or craving food, it won't make you ill or kill you if you don't eat straight away, so there's nothing to be afraid of. This is all assuming, of course, that you are not diabetic or suffering from severe under-weight due to illness or famine, or in some other situation or physical or mental condition where not eating is potentially dangerous.

Behavioural tricks which many people have found good to beat or weaken hunger or food cravings include:

- Drinking a large glass of water between meals, or immediately before or during your meal, just in case you're "hungry" for water and not food, and also to expand your stomach to help make it feel full.
- Waiting at least thirty minutes for the urge to eat to subside.
- Putting a physical obstacle between you and the food you crave.
- Chewing some sugar-free gum.
- Brushing and flossing your teeth.

Cognitive tricks include:

- Reminding yourself assertively that it's *just* a hunger, desire or craving, and that you don't *need* to eat; you won't get ill or die.

- Being strict and firm with yourself about absolutely,

definitely and most certainly *not* giving in to any temptation.

- When temptation looms, making some positive assertions to yourself, such as "I don't eat dessert" or "I choose not to snack in the evening" or "I will only eat a starter and main course at the restaurant." Make your phrases healthy, personal, based on choice, deliberate, purposeful, life-affirming, and empowering to your mind. Actively avoid using the more unhealthy phrases that are disempowering and conform to external expectations of others like "I can't …" or "I should…" or "I ought…"

- Reminding yourself that resisting hunger, desire and craving *now* has the benefit that it will increase your tolerance later on, so that future pangs of hunger and cravings will be less intense and come less often. Also, you will become more confident of your ability to resist, and your willpower "muscles" will become stronger, too.

- Challenging yourself with questions like "Am I really hungry?" and "Do I really need to eat this?" and "I don't really need to eat right now, and my next meal isn't so far off that I'll get ill, wither away and starve to death if I don't eat right now".

- Reminding yourself why you want to learn to withstand temptations, listing off all your reasons for wanting to lose weight and stay fit and slim.

- Distracting yourself from your feelings of hunger with something you really enjoy doing – and something creative if you can – such as enjoyable work, writing, reading, chatting, listening to an audiobook or podcast or radio, watching TV or something on the web, surfing the internet, going for a walk, going for a drive, meditating, playing a game, doing some vigorous exercise, or taking a bath or shower.

- Playing the freely-available tile-matching puzzle game Tetris on your computer or smartphone for just three minutes has been shown to significantly reduce cravings for food.

- Feeding off your guilt, shame and regret instead of food – reminding yourself how awful you'll feel about yourself if you give in to the temptation to eat now for just a brief time of pleasure, just like you did in the past, and how good you'll feel if you resist.

- Reminding yourself about all the starving people around the world who have little or no choice when to eat or not, and of the estimated 20,000 of whom die every single day of hunger and starvation, with one child dying every ten seconds due to starvation. These utterly dreadful figures should make all of us who eat too much ashamed of ourselves.

- Vividly imagining something really gross that will put you off your food, such as someone really ugly or otherwise repulsive (or some smelly dog) licking, sneezing, dribbling or spitting on your food; or imagine flies, maggots, slugs, worms and other slimy-oozy things you can't actually see crawling around inside the food. Be disgustingly creative here.

Bite-Size Tip #60

Getting Back on Track – Dealing with Slip-Ups and Setbacks

It is almost certain that you will have occasional slip-ups and set-backs in your weight-loss progress. This is totally normal and should be expected. What you need to do is have plans in place to help you deal with such events so as to reduce their damage and help you get back on track as soon as possible.

You need to be especially careful of falling into the "What the Hell" trap. Examples of this all-or-nothing, black-and-white mindset are when you've eaten more than you planned and think something along the lines of:

> "Oh well, since I cheated a little, what the hell, I may as well eat whatever I want for the rest of the day/weekend/week. I'll just get back on to my diet after that"

or how about

> "Oh well, since I've just eaten a few biscuits and ruined my diet for the day, well, what the hell, I may as well polish off the whole pack"

and then there's the

> "Since I've eaten a few spoonfuls of this lovely, delicious ice cream straight from the tub, well, what the hell, I may as well just polish off the whole tub; after all, no one's looking, there's not THAT much left in the tub, and I can just get back on track with my diet plan tomorrow".

Instead, the very best thing you can do when you slip-up is simply:

- STOP over-indulging there and then, right NOW.

- Accept that you made a mistake which on its own won't make that much difference to your weight-loss across the week; in other words, it's no big deal.

- DO NOT wait until "tomorrow" to get back on your diet plan; in other words, get back on your diet plan immediately, right NOW, this very moment, at once;

- Don't indulge in any feelings of failure, helplessness, reproach or deep guilt; it's really no big deal and we all slip up now and again.

- Think of a very clear and preferably physical way of signalling to yourself that you have drawn a line under the little slip-up, and are now back fully on your diet plan. Such a signal might be to clean your teeth, take a shower, go out for a walk, take a nap, call a friend for a chat – or do the whole lot – or engage in some other non-eating-related physical activity, all the while telling yourself that this activity is a sign that you are now back on your diet, with all systems go.

- As an afterthought, you might also think about what you can learn from the mistake and how you might avoid it next time.

Now move on.

Bite-Size Tip 61
How to Deal With a Weight Plateau

However well you stick to your weight-loss plan, and even if you lose no more than about half a pound or one pound of fat each week, then sooner or later your average rate of weight-loss will slow down, finally reaching a point where your weight pretty much plateaus and stabilizes without going down any further. This is a weight plateau.

Short-term weight plateaus of a few days to a week or so are a normal part of weight-loss for most people, at least in the first few months of dieting, and should be expected. So they are no cause for worry. What we are concerned with here are longer-term weight plateaus of weeks or months. This longer-term plateauing or levelling off of your weight is because of the way your body adapts and changes its energy usage, or rate of metabolism, to your new lower calorie intake. In effect, your body slows things down in such a way that you actually need less energy or fewer calories to keep things going than you did before you started dieting and exercising.

So, what do you do if you arrive at one of those seemingly relentless, long-term plateaus, where your weight seems to stick on pretty much the same amount day after day and week after week, despite you being very strict and constant with your calorie intake and exercise?

There are a number of things you can do, pretty much in the following order:

1. Don't change your diet or exercise plans at all for the moment, for at least another two or three weeks, just to see if your weight starts to fall again. Maybe it's still just a temporary plateau due to some reason you're not consciously aware of, such as hormonal changes or something external like the weather, the season, work or home life.

2. If after trying Option 1 your weight plateau has stayed the same for at least two or three more weeks, you can choose to reduce your daily calorie intake a little more by, say, two hundred or so calories. Obviously, this is not an option if you started your diet by cutting your calorie intake to the safe minimum of daily calories anyway.

3. Instead of, or as well as Option 2, you could increase your daily or weekly fat-burning exercise – such as longer or more frequent brisk walks, more time puffing-and-panting with cardio-vascular exercise, or maybe more weight training. Obviously, if you're not doing any fat-burning exercise at all worth talking about right now, just like many unhealthy dieters don't, then you might think about starting an exercise programme at this point.

4. If you don't want to drop your calories or up your exercises, then you need to mentally and emotionally adjust your expectations, and just resign yourself to the fact that you have probably reached your minimum healthily *maintainable* weight, and so you now need to shift your attention onto *maintaining* the weight-loss you've achieved to date rather than struggling to reduce it even more.

In conclusion, it's wiser not to expect to lose weight every single week. Instead, your weight will plateau off from time to time for one reason or another, even if you are sticking strictly to your eating and exercise plans. It is better to assume that you will sometimes lose weight for a week or two, sometimes plateau off for a week or two, and sometimes even put weight back on again. And you just have to acknowledge and accept that sooner or later your weight will level off and plateau for the long-term, especially when you reach your final lowest easily maintainable weight.

Bite-Size Tip 62

What if You Can't Maintain Your Desired Target Weight?

Sooner or later your rate of weight loss will begin to slow down and plateau off, and your weight will pretty much stabilize. This happens even when you carry on eating the same healthy lowest amount of calories possible, and while you keep up the same amount of any physical exercise. It's at this point you will have reached your healthy lowest *achievable* weight, which will only go lower if you unhealthily eat even less or vigorously exercise even more, or both; not recommended.

The problem is that most people find it just too hard, or even impossible, over the long term to keep on eating the same reduced number of calories, while exercising by the same amount, to stay at their lowest *achievable* weight for the rest of their lives. Even with the very best of intentions, because they are eating and exercising at unsustainable levels for them, what usually happens is that they sooner or later start eating a little more, and often start exercising less too, and so their weight slowly creeps back up by at least a few pounds before plateauing off and stabilising again at a higher level.

The important thing here is to set a plan for eating, drinking and exercise that you're genuinely happy with, a plan that you can comfortably stick to, and so maintain for the rest of your life. It's at this point that you will have reached your very own lowest *maintainable* weight, which will be at least a few pounds heavier than your unsustainable lowest *achievable* weight.

Some people are at first not happy with their heavier body-shape when they plateau at their lowest maintainable weight. To become happy enough with it, here are ten ways of thinking about it:

- Learn to be *satisfied enough* with your lowest maintainable weight, not least because you can't sensibly or easily do much about it anyway. So it's best to just learn to accept yourself as you are, warts, fat and all.

- Remind yourself how much easier and agreeable it is to stick to your lowest maintainable weight rather than to your lowest achievable weight, which will require a lot more painful effort to stick to.

- Remember that you can at least temporarily get back down to your lowest achievable weight again if you need to for some good reason, not least because you managed it before.

- Acknowledge how well you've done to reach your lowest maintainable weight, and all the benefits you've reaped as a result, based on your list of reasons for wanting to slim down in the first place.

- Pretend you are at your ideal weight, vividly and strongly acting as if your lowest maintainable weight is actually your ideal lowest achievable weight. If you continually act as if your lowest maintainable weight is indeed your ideal weight, you'll eventually stop pretending and will actually start to really believe it too, and so you will become happy enough with your lowest maintainable weight after all (I did).

- When you step on the weighing machine, it's just nicer and easier to measure your weight that day against your lowest maintainable weight, which, by definition, is easier to stick to.

- Focus more on other aspects of yourself that please you, rather than on the parts of your body that may still look and feel a little too fat for your liking. For example, you might well have a lovely face and smile, or you might be attractive and sexy regardless or even because of the slight excess of fat you're still storing – perhaps you are curvy and voluptuous. You might also focus more on positive aspects of your personality: maybe you are clever and intelligent, or have a great sense of humour, or are really kind and compassionate, or enjoyable company to be with, or all these things combined.

- If being physically attractive and especially being sexy is important to you, remember that how you look is only part of the formula. Sexiness is as much to do with how you behave, such as "what you do with what you've got".

- Stop comparing yourself to wrong things such as people around you or what you believe to be the standards and expectations of your social group or the wider society you live in, including what you see in glossy magazines and clothes catalogues. Stop comparing yourself too with Hollywood or TV actors: on screen and at celebrity events they're all make-believe anyway. Be authentic, the best version of yourself that you can be.

- Enrich and enhance your life in as many different ways as you can – many people eat too much because they are not contented or fulfilled, often because they are not meeting their fundamental human needs. The richer, more fulfilled, more contented and happier you can make your life, in all aspects, then the less you'll focus on your weight and how you look, and so you'll be more than happy enough to have achieved your minimum maintainable weight.

Bite-Size Tip 63

Beware those Negative Naysayers

You will probably come across some people who are unhelpful, discouraging and otherwise unsupportive to your weight-loss efforts. These people do so consciously or unconsciously, with good intentions or bad. Either way, these are your naysayers, and they come in various shapes and sizes, quite literally.

Naysayers might be friends, relatives, colleagues or loved-ones who tell you, quite genuinely, that they don't think you need to lose weight and that you shouldn't. Or naysayers may be fellow dieters who don't always give you the feedback you need, particularly when you're feeling bad about yourself after a slip-up or set-back, especially when they have slipped up similarly themselves.

Alternatively, naysayers may be fat people in your close social group who discourage you from losing weight because, consciously or unconsciously, they want you to stay fat like them.

In fact, there is a passive or unconscious "naysayer influence" if you spend a lot of time in a social group of mainly non-dieting fat people whom, at some deep, unconscious level, you want to be like because you want to be a part of their group. Then there is the naysayer who offers you food – even psychologically or physically forces food upon you – often with the guilt-inducing comment, after they place the uninvited dish in front of you: 'I made it especially for you!' (Mothers and mothers-in-law come to mind here.)

Finally there is the more unpleasant, toxic breed of naysayer, albeit rare, one hopes, who delights in criticising and even ridiculing your weight-loss plans or achievements. They come up with sneering comments, often through pseudo-friendly smiles, saying things like, "You? ... Lose weight? ... What, like all the other times you dieted? ... Who are you fooling? ... Don't make me laugh? ... Have another cake ..."All naysayer cases, whether well-intentioned or not, can, if you let them, erode your motivation and resolve to succeed with your weight-loss plans.

To reduce the negative influence of naysayers, affirm to yourself the following statements:

- I have every right to work at losing weight if that's my choice, for whatever reason, as long as I'm not intentionally and maliciously trying to make other fat people around me feel bad about themselves. If they do feel bad about themselves because of my weight-loss activities, particularly my successes, then that's unfortunate, but it's their responsibility to deal with this issue, and not mine.

- My reasons for wanting to lose weight are individual and personal to my own health and wellbeing, as they should be, and have absolutely nothing to do with the health and wellbeing of other people, however fat they are. So I will strive not to compare my weight-loss results with those of others, and, if I do, I will always strive to make any comparisons positive and supportive to my own and others' efforts.

- It's OK to disappoint other people who want to feed me – however genuinely nice and generous they are being towards me – as long as I do so politely and sensitively, and even firmly if need be. It's totally up to me how much I want to eat, and I have no need to feel guilty in any way about other people's expectations, or disappointment at my polite refusal to eat all they are offering me.

- After all, what about my disappointment at myself if I accept all the food they want to pile on me and so stray from my eating plan? And if I make them aware of my weight-loss goals, should they not be considerate to my wishes? And why should it be more important for me to please them than it is to stay on my eating plan to please me (unless they're about to sign over their multi-million pound estate to me, of course)? If they really do care about me in any way, their disappointment will almost certainly be mild and fleeting anyway. If not, hard luck. Get over it.

- I'm absolutely entitled to feel fine about turning down food offers from other people, especially when I keep in mind the emotional and physical costs to me of accepting, which include:
    - going off my personal eating plans; eating more than I really want;
    - feeling that I'll have to deny myself later to offset eating now;
    - feeling out of control, even in a small way;
    - stopping losing weight or even gaining some weight;
    - feeling bad about myself for eating when my diet plan told me not to.

- Unpleasant, overtly critical and unhelpful people – especially those of malicious intent – can go to Hell in a handcart for all I care about their ill-informed opinions. Idiots!

You might find it helpful to rehearse your responses to potential naysayers in advance. Finally, telling naysayers that you are losing weight for "health reasons" almost always stops them in their tracks, since they can't reasonably deny the many proven health benefits of shedding excess fat.

Bite-Size Tip 64
Eat Slowly and Mindfully

Many studies show that people who eat quickly tend to be heavier and gain more weight than slower eaters. Put another way, fat people tend to chew their food *less* than thinner people do. So if you want to lose weight, eat your meal more slowly and chew your food more. Chewing your food thoroughly slows down your pace of eating and reduces the number of calories you take in, because you feel fuller after eating less food.

There are several benefits to eating slowly:

- **It helps you lose weight** – it gives your brain more time to notice when you've eaten enough for your needs.
- **You'll enjoy your food more** – you'll have more time to savour the textures, tastes, aromas and overall flavours.
- **Smaller meals become satisfying** – eating more slowly makes you feel full without eating so much.
- **It's better for your digestion** – chewing food into smaller fragments makes them easier to digest.
- **It helps relieve indigestion, acid reflux and gastroesophageal reflux disease (GERD)** – more efficient digestion needs less digestive juices.
- **It can reduce stress** – eating more slowly can make you feel calmer, less stressed, and more in control.
- **It can improve your dental health** – chewing more slowly puts less stress on your teeth and gums.
- **It's good exercise for your jaw muscles** – more chewing equals more exercise for your jaw muscles.
- **It can reduce health risks** – it can lower your risk of diabetes, metabolic syndrome and insulin resistance.

There are a number of ways in which you can eat more slowly:

- **Chew more slowly** – open and close your jaws more slowly, in slower-motion.
- **Chew more times** – maybe between twenty and forty times, or at least twice as many times as you used to, or for twice as long. But just be aware that chewing each mouthful of food too many times can spoil your enjoyment of the meal, so be sensible.
- **Take smaller bites** – this means it can take longer to finish your meal because you need to take more bites.
- **Serve your food boiling hot** – people usually eat very hot food more slowly, giving it time to cool.
- **Put utensils down between bites** – this generally slows down your pace of eating; it's more relaxing, too.
- **Drink a *small* sip of water every one or two bites** – this slows your overall pace of eating.
- **Eat small things like nuts, berries or grapes one at a time** – again, this slows your overall pace of eating.
- **Time yourself to eat slowly** – for example, allow up to twice as long to eat your meal.
- **Leave generous time gaps between courses** – giving your brain more time to notice the food coming in.
- **Eat with the "wrong" hand** – this usually forces you to at least put the food into your mouth more slowly.
- **Take a few deep breaths between mouthfuls** – this slows your overall pace of eating.
- **Don't allow yourself to get too hungry** – hungry people are more likely to eat too much, too quickly.
- **Play an "ingredients spotting" game while chewing** – taking time chewing each bite makes this easier.
- **Sit down at a table to eat** – people who don't sit down at a table usually eat too fast, partly because they're not relaxed, feel rushed or are distracted from eating their food slowly for some other reason.
- **Don't do anything which distracts you from your slow eating** – otherwise you risk eating too quickly.
- **Chat with people sitting and eating with you** – if you

are eating in company, stop eating when someone is talking to you, perhaps putting your utensils down, and, of course, don't talk with your mouth full.

- **Eat slower than the slowest eater in your company** – as long as they normally eat slower than you, of course.

- **Think deeply about what you're eating: eat "mindfully"** – this is where you pay very close, focused attention on just eating your meal, which itself helps you to eat more slowly and eat less. Mindful eating involves full awareness of what you're eating while you're eating it, so the idea is to stay in the "here and now" while you eat. It is a lot easier to do when you're free of all other distractions so you can focus your attention fully on the food and the present moment. Arguably, eating in silence is the best way to eat mindfully, if you can manage it. Obviously, this is not something to practise if you are at a social event or a dinner party!

Whatever slow-eating techniques you use to help you eat less, the mindset of eating slowly is a habit that needs to be acquired and practiced over time, again and again. You almost certainly won't pick it up overnight. Remember that any cognitive or behavioural change takes time, sometimes weeks or even months. But altering your old, faster eating habits in the ways described will certainly help. So don't give up, but keep going with your slow-eating practice, and you will succeed in time. If you keep on, eating slowly will become easier, natural and more sustainable for you.

Bite-Size Tip 65
Practise Portion Control

Poor portion control can be a barrier to losing weight, and is often overlooked. One of the problems here is how much it *looks* like we're eating. Studies show that we're more likely to feel full up if it *looks* like we've eaten enough.

Another problem with portion control is habit. We get used to eating certain amounts, including making sure we eat our plates clean. That's why many of us tend to almost always prepare pretty much the same amount of food for a meal, regardless of how hungry we feel, and we usually eat all of it, too!

So to help with your weight-loss, you need to get some conscious control over the amount of food and calorie-loaded drinks you serve yourself.

If you have sufficiently strong willpower, you may find that gaining control over portion sizes isn't too difficult. To give you some help here, I've written a whole section in this guide on how to improve your willpower (see Bite-Size Tip 51: Strengthen Your Willpower Muscles for a summary). But there are some things you can do which help to actually reduce the amount of willpower you'll need (see Tip 52: Get More Motivated and Tip 53: Break Bad Habits and Hone Healthy Habits).

Most obviously, you could start out just by eating and drinking *only slightly* smaller portions. For instance, when it comes to your meals at home, you could measure the amounts of food you have prepared for yourself up until now, and then cut the amount by just ten percent, or one-tenth. If you cut down by such a small amount, you're less likely to notice when you come to eat it, either visually on the plate or from a "hunger satisfaction" point of view. When you get used to eating about ten percent less than you used to, cut the amount again by just a tiny bit more if you feel the need, again being careful to make sure you don't reduce so much that either your eyes or your stomach will notice it.

Also, it can be much easier to eat and drink smaller portions if you reduce the size of your crockery, too, so that you are serving smaller amounts. This is a visual illusion, helping your brain think that you've had enough and are satisfied once you've emptied the plates or bowls, pretty much as it did when you polished off the contents of *slightly* larger crockery.

Studies have shown that most people do, indeed, find smaller portions more satisfying if they eat and drink from *slightly* smaller crockery. When I say "*slightly* smaller", I do mean "*just a bit*" smaller, at least at first. In the case of dinner plates, this is easy because they usually come in different sizes. The same often goes for bowls, too. Most importantly, what I *don't* mean is eating your whole main meal from, say, a small side plate or little dessert-size bowl. These would be so obviously small to your eyes that there's no way you'll be able to fool your brain visually that you've eaten enough, not least because you almost certainly wouldn't have from such a small plate or bowl.

That said, when it comes to a meal that has two or more different parts in the same course – such as meat, potatoes, and two or three vegetables – you might well try serving each part on its own small side-plate or bowl. If you place them all on the table in front of you at the same time, the chances are it'll look and feel like a veritable feast.

As a final tip here, it will be easier to get into the healthy habit of eating smaller portion sizes if you adopt other healthy eating habits that I describe elsewhere in this guide, especially eating more slowly (for a summary see Bite-Size Tip 64: Eat Slowly and Mindfully).

Bite-Size Tip 66
Ask for Help if You Need It

Are you finding it hard to lose weight on your own? If so, you're not alone. Studies show that very few people who struggle with dieting can lose weight, and keep if off long-term, without some form of help and encouragement from a person or a group of people. A genuinely trusted and supportive confidant – or a group of people – can make you more motivated and committed to stick to making changes and promises of action – or action commitments – that will achieve your weight-loss goal.

Probably the best benefit of getting help from other people in this way is that they can keep you accountable for your weight-loss goals, plans and actions. Here's how:

1. First write down your specific weight-loss goal in as much detail as you can, including points such as:

    - why you really do want to lose weight
    - what being slim will do for you
    - what your target weight is
    - why you think it's an achievable and realistic target
    - when you plan to reach it

Include any interim goals, such as:

    - losing so many pounds by such and such a date
    - what specific eating and exercise actions and habits you'll commit to do in order to achieve your goal
    - the sort of obstacles and barriers you expect to encounter along the way
    - what you can do about them

2. You then need to keep an accurate and honest record of your progress as you go along.

3. Send all your written details from steps 1 and 2 to a non-judgemental and supportive friend or group. It's especially important to include all your action commitments, and, in your regular progress reports, you should include any obstacles, difficulties or slip-ups you've had along the way. You need to send all this on at least a weekly basis, I would say. Your trusted confidant should want to see on-going commitment and progress from you, and they can help you keep in focus how far you've moved towards reaching your weight-loss goal and how far you have left to go.

Other key benefits of getting support from other people:

- they can help you to become clear about your weight-loss goals, plans and action steps – just going through the above three steps with them can achieve this. This is especially true if you actually speak to your helper about everything you have in mind, without at first getting any comments or feedback from them. Speaking out loud, even just to yourself, can aid creative thinking and problem-solving.

- they can help you to keep motivated – by reminding you of all your reasons for wanting to lose weight and the benefits you'll reap from being slimmer.

- they can help you to solve problems – especially those to do with overcoming obstacles, barriers and temptations.

- they can help you to make decisions even when they are not there – when you're being sorely tempted, or when your resolve feels weak, imagine your helper looking over your shoulder. At these times, when you know what you should do but you're having trouble doing it, ask yourself, 'What would my supportive helper say to me now?'

- they can help you to build your self-confidence – such as by acknowledging your progress and achievements to date, including all the obstacles and temptations you've overcome.

- they can help you to feel part of a supportive group – this is an often-unacknowledged, fundamental human need of almost all people; don't neglect it or undervalue its worth for you.

So who can help you to lose weight? There are at least five options worth considering:

- A weekly slimming club
- A trusted friend, relative or colleague
- A professional weight-loss coach
- A psychotherapist or counsellor – especially if you feel that you got fat, or are finding it too difficult to lose weight, because of some deeper, underlying mental health or emotional problem that you're having trouble managing on your own
- An imaginary friend, group, coach or other "helper"; be they real, fictional or mythical; from past or present; animate or inanimate; animal, vegetable or mineral. Anything's possible in the realm of the imagination

Regardless of whoever – or whatever – you choose to enlist, getting help with your weight-loss goals and plans can greatly increase your chances of success, particularly if you're having problems losing weight on your own. At the very least, a supportive individual or group of any sort – real or imaginary – is someone to whom you can submit all of your weight-loss goals, plans and progress reports on a regular basis (as outlined in steps 1 to 3 earlier), without fear of negative judgment or criticism. But more than that, a "real" supportive individual or group can, in one way or another, also offer you on-going and much-needed support and encouragement when things get tough, which you must assume they will from time to time. They can help you identify and counter any unhelpful thinking, can encourage and motivate you, and may be able to offer practical advice and guidance when you feel stuck. If nothing else, a supportive helper will, by definition, be willing to help you in whatever way they can, even if they only act as a sounding board to help you clarify your own thoughts, feelings and actions – even a totally imaginary helper can do that.

Would You Like "Dr Mark" to Help You Lose Weight?

In writing this book, and the associated multi-media material on the website, I sincerely hope that my readers, listeners and viewers will have all the information they need to be able to successfully reach and maintain their weight-loss goals.

However, if you feel that you would like some help in achieving your weight-loss goals, and don't fancy the idea of joining a weight-loss group or confiding in a trusted friend, then please do get in touch with me via the website if you do fancy the idea of engaging me to be your very own Weight-Loss Coach and Mentor. As the author of this Diet Tricks guide, and as a qualified cognitive-behavioural coach and mentor, I'd like to think that I know my stuff here, and should be able to help if you're willing.

That said, I'd like to point out that because of other ongoing commitments, I can only work with two or three clients at any given time. But it's worth getting in touch to see if or when I'm available for you, and to explore the coaching and mentoring options I can offer you, along with the associated costs.

I'm happy to work with clients face-to-face, or remotely via telephone or via internet phone/video calls.

Twelve More Tricks of Thinking and Behaving That Can Help You Lose Weight

I first got the idea to write this book when I started collecting lots of what I call "cognitive and behavioural tricks". They are ways of thinking, feeling and behaving – usually fun, novel or even a bit strange – which people can use to help them to change things in their lives; in this case to change the way they think, feel and behave around eating (and exercise) to help them lose weight. In many respects, that is how my eventual written work evolved, and so this book does contain lots of so-called "tricks" throughout, though there are lots more in the more detailed information in Part 2 of my Diet Tricks guide, accessible on the associated website (www. DietTricks.com).

But just for a bit of fun, novelty and even strangeness right here and now, I thought I'd include twelve of the sort of "tricks" I originally wanted to write a whole book about. Two or three of the tricks which follow are included in the more detailed Part 2, but most are not. They are all scientifically-based, have worked for other people, and so may work for you, too.

Over time I intend to include the details of many such weight-loss tricks – including those here – on the– website, so do subscribe if you are interested.

Thinking (Cognitive) Tricks

67. **Pledging money to hated organisations if you fail**
    Threaten to give money to a hated cause or organisation if you fail to reach a particular weight-loss goal.

68. **Look in the mirror while you prepare food**
    Hang a large mirror in the kitchen where you can see yourself out of the corner of your eyes preparing food, especially from the waist upwards.

69. **Eat where it's quiet**
    Avoid loud noises while you eat; loud noises can make you eat more.

70. **Imagine what you eat will make you fat**
    If you don't want to eat too much in a particular meal, strongly imagine everything you're eating is really fattening, and so it will make you really fat.

71. **Remember past satisfying meals if you feel hungry now**
    If you're feeling a bit peckish, remembering vividly when you ate satisfying meals in the past can actually satisfy your peckishness now.

72. **Dream about losing weight**
    Vividly thinking about your weight-loss goal and plans as you drift off to sleep can help you lose weight when you're awake.

Behavioural Tricks

73. **Don't empty your plate**
Leaving a little food on your plate or bowl when you want to stop eating sends a message to your brain that you have eaten enough.

74. **Push your plate or bowl away from you when you want to stop eating**
Works like not emptying your plate.

75. **Close your eyes (and ears) when chewing**
Helps you savour food more, which can be more satisfying, because without sight (or hearing) you'll pay more attention to tastes, smells, flavours and textures.

76. **Brush your teeth when you feel hungry**
Many people brush their teeth after eating and so they don't feel they should eat immediately after brushing – brushing your teeth uses a few calories too!

77. **Look at pictures of food**
Although it sounds counter-intuitive, looking at lots of pictures of food one after the other can weaken or remove hunger.

78. **Make a multi-purpose weight-loss charm, talisman and amulet**
Acquire or make something small which symbolises to your mind your weight-loss goal and endeavours. Perhaps consider an attractive gemstone, crystal or piece of jewellery. It doesn't have to be expensive but it might be more "powerful" if it is. Always carry it with you. Handle and look at it to remind yourself of all the whys and wherefores of your weight-loss endeavours. Handle it especially whenever you feel the temptation to eat when you'd rather not. You can think of it as a sort of charm to attract good luck on your diet, an amulet to protect

you from the dangers of those foody temptations, and a talisman to attract all the benefits of being slimmer.

Concluding Thoughts

Well, there you have it. Some of the very best tips, tools and techniques of thinking, feeling and behaving you can have a go at to help you lose weight, just like I did. They probably won't all work well for you, if at all, but enough will. And the more tips you have a go at, the more likely you'll be successful in reaching and maintaining your weight-loss goal. It's that simple.

With any luck, you'll have more than enough in this book alone to help you achieve your wildest weight-loss dreams. As a real bonus, I also hope you'll work out for yourself how you can use lots of the tips in this book to help you achieve other things in your life too, just as the main title implies. Just remember that there are lots more practical ideas to be found on the associated website (www. DietTricks.com).

Lots of the material on the website will be free for you to access, especially if you have this book to hand, as you'll need some information from it for access passwords; so don't lose it or give it away to some other fat person (tell them to buy their own copy, the sluggards).

Parts 2 and 3 of the Diet Tricks Guide: a Synopsis

All the contents of Parts 2 and 3 can be found on the associated website: www.DietTricks.com.

Part 2: The Main Course

More information about Tips 21 to 68 that are summarized in this book.

Topic 1: Losing Weight Has to Matter a Lot to You Personally

21. **Keep an Accurate Record of Everything**
    An Often-Quoted Study
    The Good News
    Writing by Hand
    Choose Between a Journal, Sheet Paper or Computer
    Use Pictures, Diagrams, Tables and Graphs
    Use Lots of Colour
    Choose an Inspiring Title
    Some Final Thoughts
22. **You Need to Really Want to Lose Weight Badly Enough**
    A Smoker's Story
    My Story: Why Losing Weight Mattered to Me Enough –
        Eventually
    FAT FACT: Can You Be Fat *and* Fit?
23. **Make Sure You Want to Get Slim for the Right Personal Reasons**

24. **Make Sure Losing Weight Meets Your Fundamental Human Needs**
What Are Our Fundamental Human Needs?
Is There a Hierarchy of Human Needs?
How Might You Not Be Satisfying Your Fundamental
    Human Needs?
Satisfying Our Fundamental Human Needs
A Metaphor or Two About Life-Balance
Real-Life Examples From My Life
Our Fundamental Needs Motivate Us to Act
Fundamental Needs and Losing Weight
25. **List All the Consequences of Losing Weight and Being Slim, Both to You and to Other People**
26. **Identify Your *True Reason* for Wanting To Lose Weight**
Needing Money
Use the "Downward Arrow Technique" to Help Discover
    Your True Reasons
What is the Downward Arrow Technique?
Using the Downward Arrow Technique to Help You
    Lose Weight
Using the Downward Arrow Technique:
    Example 1 – My High Cholesterol Problem
    Example 2 – Feeling Bad About Being Fat
27. **Expect to Make Long-Term Lifestyle Changes**
28. **Expect to Struggle – But Prepare to Beat It**
29. **Be Kind and Compassionate to Yourself About Your Body (*W*)**
Being Kind and Compassionate About Myself
30. **Don't Look to Lose Weight to Make You Feel Happier with Your Life Generally**

Topic 2: What is Your Weight-Loss Goal?

31. **Make Your Weight-Loss Goal Positive and Result-Oriented**
A Fast Story
A Psychological Law of Attraction

Nurture?

Self-Worth and Fundamental Human Needs

Cultivating and Maintaining a Healthy Sense of Self
Worth

How I Further Cultivated and Maintained a Healthy
Sense of Self-Worth

Low Self-Worth Doesn't Mean You Won't Be Able to
Achieve Things

Self-Worth, Self-Esteem and Self-Efficacy Are
All Necessary

On Self-Acceptance

40. **If You Have Doubts, then "Fake It Till You Make It" or
"Act As If" You Can Lose Weight**

41. **Make Sure Your Weight-Loss Goal Is Really Relevant to
You Personally**

42. **Define When You Want to Reach Your Target Weight**

43. **Focus on How Far You've Got to Go to Reach Your
Weight-Loss Goal, Not on How Far You've Come**

44. **Your Weight-Loss Goal Statement Should Stimulate
Multi-Sensory Thinking and Emotions**

Visualising, "Sensorising" and "Emotionalising"
Getting Slimmer

Creative Visualisation

Emotions Motivate

Buying Cars and Watches

Your Sensorised and Emotionalised Weight-Loss
Goal Statement

Topic 3: What are the Obstacles that Stop You Getting Slim?

45. **Identify the Navigable Obstacles and Barriers**

46. **Monitor those Eating "Triggers"**

47. **Use "Back From the Future" Thinking**

48. **Plan in Advance to Replace an Unhelpful Triggered
Behaviour With a Helpful One**

Introducing "If-Then" Implementation Intention Planning

Willpower versus Motivation
53. **Break Bad Habits and Hone Healthy Habits**
Running on Autopilot
Cleaning Teeth
Slapping Walls
Pointless Gasping
The Definition of a Habit
Acquiring a New Habit Can Take Some Time
All About Your Habits
How to Change Your Habits
54. **Prepare For Red for Danger Days**
55. **Lose Weight to Gain Weight (*W*)**
56. **Use Mental Rehearsal to Prepare for Challenging Situations**
Mental Rehearsal and Sport
Can Your Brain Tell the Difference Between Real
    and Imagined Events?
Remembering Things With Mental Rehearsal
Using Mental Rehearsal With Our Willpower and Habits
A Worry-Busting Aside
57. **Feed on Guilt, Shame and Regret**
58. **Are You *Really* Hungry? (*W*)**
Some People Don't Get Hungry
Only Eat When You Feel Hungry?
Some People Think They're Hungry When They're Not
What to Do if You Can't Tell the Difference?
How to Recognise Metabolic Hunger
How to Recognise Hedonic or Emotional Hunger
Early Time-Restricted Feeding
59. **Learn to Tolerate Hunger, Desire and Craving (*W*)**
Not Eating Won't Kill You
Behavioural Ways to Beat Hunger, Desire and Craving
Cognitive Ways to Beat Hunger, Desire and Craving
60. **Getting Back on Track – Dealing With Slip-Ups and Setbacks**
Watch-Out for the "What the Hell" Trap
Ignore Conventional Time Divisions
Don't Overestimate the Seriousness of Your Slip-Up

Part 3: Why You Eat the Way You Do

Would You Like "Dr Mark" to Help You Lose Weight?

In writing this book, and the associated multi-media material on the website, I sincerely hope that my readers, listeners and viewers will have all the information they need to be able to successfully reach and maintain their weight-loss goals.

However, if you feel that you would like some help in achieving your weight-loss goals, and don't fancy the idea of joining a weight-loss group or confiding in a trusted friend, then please do get in touch with me via the website if you do fancy the idea of engaging me to be your very own Weight-Loss Coach and Mentor. As the author of this Diet Tricks guide, and as a qualified cognitive-behavioural coach and mentor, I'd like to think that I know my stuff here, and should be able to help if you're willing.

That said, I'd like to point out that because of other ongoing commitments, I can only work with two or three clients at any given time. But it's worth getting in touch to see if or when I'm available for you, and to explore the coaching and mentoring options I can offer you, along with the associated costs.

I'm happy to work with clients face-to-face, or remotely via telephone or via internet phone/video calls.

Index

Other Books by Mark Biddiss (a.k.a. "Dr Mark")

Science Books

1. Dr Mark's MAGICAL SCIENCE
   A Set of Fun & Novel Experiments About Physical Processes, Properties of Materials & Ourselves – Book 1
2. Dr Mark's MAGICAL SCIENCE – Book 2
3. Dr Mark's MAGICAL SCIENCE – Book 3
4. Dr Mark's CIRCUS SCIENCE
   Clowning Around With Forces, Motion, Materials & Ourselves
5. Dr Mark's SOUND OF SCIENCE at The Royal Albert Hall
   31 Amazing Curriculum-Based Experiments About the Science of Sound
6. Dr Mark's FORCES & PHYSICS
   A Set of Fun & Novel Experiments About Forces, Motion & Other Physical Processes
7. Dr Mark's MATERIALS & CHEMISTRY
   A Set of Fun & Novel Experiments About Solids, Liquids, Gases & Other Properties of Materials
8. Dr Mark's HUMANS & BIOLOGY
   A Set of Fun & Novel Experiments About Human Senses, Strength, Balance, Coordination & More!
9. Dr Mark's EXPLOSIVE EXPERIMENTS
   Brilliant & Easy Science Experiments For Kids Using Things From the Supermarket

10. Dr Mark's FUN SCIENCE PARTY BOOK
    Screaming Straws, 'Orrible Ooze, Slime & More! 10
    Explosive, Noisy, Slimy & Oozy Experiments!

Maths Books

11. Dr Mark's MAGICAL MATHS
    A Set of Fun & Novel "Mathemagical" Activities &
    "Arithmetricks" To Stimulate Problem-Solving, Reasoning &
    Communication Skills – Book 1
12. Dr Mark's MAGICAL MATHS – Book 2
13. Dr Mark's MAGICAL MATHS – Book 3
14. Dr Mark's NOVEL NUMERACY & MATHS
    A Set of Fun & Engaging Number-Based Activities to Enrich
    & Enliven Maths Teaching & Learning
15. Dr Mark's PROBLEM-SOLVING & VISUAL MATHS
    A Set of Fun & Engaging Numberless Activities to Enrich &
    Enliven Maths Teaching & Learning
16. Dr Mark's MATHEMAGIC & ARITHMETRICKS
    Lots of Fun Maths Investigations for Kids

All of the above titles are available as site-licensed and printable
pdf e-books. Contact "Dr Mark" for more details via his websites:
www.Dr-Mark.co.uk or www.DietTricks.com